A GIFT FOR

....

FROM

....

The JOURNEY of
JESUS

As told by MAX McLEAN
NARRATOR of the LISTENER'S BIBLE

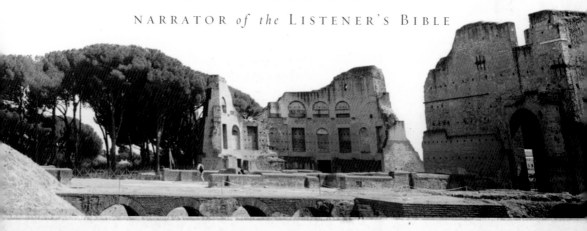

INCLUDES FULL LENGTH CD OF BIBLE STORIES

Copyright © 2006 by Max McLean

Published by J. Countryman®, a division of Thomas Nelson, Inc., Nashville, Tennessee 37214

J. Countryman® is a trademark of Thomas Nelson, Inc.

The New King James Version (NKJV) ©1979, 1980, 1982, 1992, Thomas Nelson, Inc., Publisher.
Used by permission.

The New International Version of the Bible (NIV) © 1984 by the International Bible Society. Used by permission of Zondervan Bible Publishers.

Design: studiogearbox Sisters, Oregon

Cover Image: Michael Cogliantry/Photonica

Published in association with the literary agency of Mark Sweeney & Associates, Bonita Springs, Florida 34135

Project Editor: Kathy Baker

ISBN 1 4041 0298 1

Printed and bound in China

www.thomasnelson.com www.jcountryman.com

www.listenersbible.com www.maxmclean.com

Faith comes by hearing and hearing by the word of God.

ROMANS 10:17

Listen to counsel and receive instruction,
That you may be wise in your latter days.

PROVERBS 19:20

INTRODUCTION

A baby in a manger.

A man on a cross.

These scenes are the two best-known events in the life of Jesus, but there's so much more to the story.

In this book I have selected thirty-six great stories from the gospel accounts of Jesus and retold them in simple, narrative language. Each story can be read independently in about five minutes. Yet taken together they tell one thrilling story about Jesus.

Read along as you listen to the enclosed CD of the Christmas and Easter narratives. Come walk with Jesus through these most wonderful of stories. Like his first followers, listen to the accounts of the amazing things he said and did. Hear. Believe. Let his story become your story.

"He who has ears to hear, let him hear!"

MATTHEW 13:9; MARK 4:9; LUKE 8:8

THE ANGEL IN THE TEMPLE

LUKE 1:5-25

The story of Jesus begins in the land of the Jews, called Israel, a land ruled by a king named Herod. Jerusalem was the most important city in the land of the Jews because it was the home of the great temple of God. This temple was the place where the people went to worship the God who had created the world and placed Adam and Eve in the Garden of Eden. He saved Noah from the flood and led Moses and the Israelites out of slavery in Egypt to the Promised Land where they now lived. He also gave them the Ten Commandments.

But God had not spoken to his people in a long time. After a long silence he decided to reveal what he was about to do to rescue the people of Israel and the whole world. So he sent an angel to speak to an old priest named Zechariah. This is how it happened.

One day Zechariah was leading the worship service in the temple. He was standing in front of the Most Holy Place near the great altar where sacrifices where given to God so that he would forgive the sins of the people.

Zechariah was married to a woman named Elizabeth. Both were very old and they had no children because Elizabeth was not able to have babies.

As Zechariah was doing his priestly duties behind a curtain of the temple where he could not be seen, suddenly a strange, brilliant light flashed all around him. Zechariah's heart filled with fear. The light was the angel of the Lord.

The angel spoke. "Do not be afraid of me, Zechariah. God has sent me to bring you good news. Your wife Elizabeth, who is barren, soon will have a son. You will call him John. You will be very proud of him. And he will bring you and Elizabeth great joy. God will fill him with his own Holy Spirit and he will be great in God's eyes. John will call many people in Israel to turn their inner thoughts back to the Lord. He will cause those who used to disobey the Lord to love God and do what is right."

When Zechariah heard these words, he just couldn't believe it. He told the angel: "How will I know that what you are saying is true? I am an old man and my wife is old and has never been able to have children!"

When Zechariah said this, the angel's tone changed because he was displeased that Zechariah did not believe him. "My name is Gabriel. I am the archangel. I live every day in the presence of God. The Lord himself sent me to bring you this news. But since you do not believe what I say, you will not be able to speak until all that I have promised comes to pass."

Now the people outside were wondering why Zechariah was staying so long behind the curtain. When he finally came out, they saw that he could not speak. So he made signs with his hands to them to tell them what had just happened.

When his wife Elizabeth heard what had happened in the temple and found out that God was going to give her a child, she believed. She took a moment to thank God because the news made her so wonderfully happy that now at last God would give her a child of her own.

THE ANGEL VISITS
A YOUNG GIRL NAMED MARY

LUKE 1:26-80

Six months after the angel Gabriel appeared to Zechariah, the Lord sent him to a little town called Nazareth to find a young girl named Mary. Mary was Elizabeth's cousin and she was soon to be married to a carpenter named Joseph.

The angel came into the room where Mary was sitting and said to her, "Greetings, Mary. The Lord is greatly pleased with you."

Mary was frightened and did not understand what the angel meant. Then the angel said, "Do not be afraid, Mary. The Lord has chosen you to be the mother of his Son who he will send into the world. His name will be Jesus because the Lord has sent him to save his people from their sins. He will be great and will be called the Son of the Most High God. The Lord will make him king over the people of God forever. His rule will never end."

But Mary wondered innocently about this and asked, "How can this be? I am a virgin. I have never known a man."

The angel said to her: "The Holy Spirit will come to you, and you will conceive this holy child. He will be in your womb, and in due time you will give birth to the Son of God."

Then the angel told Mary that her barren cousin Elizabeth was going to give birth to a special child in her old age.

When Mary heard this, she said, "I am the Lord's servant. May it happen to me just as you have said."

When the angel had gone, Mary got up immediately and went to visit Elizabeth and Zechariah in Jerusalem. When Elizabeth saw Mary, the baby in her womb leaped with joy, and Elizabeth said, "Blessed are you among women, and blessed be your Son!"

Then Mary, filled with the Spirit, praised God and said. "From now on people everywhere will call me blessed." Mary stayed with Elizabeth until the time her cousin gave birth.

When Elizabeth's baby was born, everyone wanted to name him Zechariah after his father. But his mother said, "No, his name is John."

"Why?" they said. "No one in your family has ever had that name."

So they asked Zechariah what name he wished to give the child. He asked for something to write upon, and when they brought it, he wrote, "His name is John."

At once Zechariah was able to speak. He praised God for the son God had given to him. He said of the boy: "You, my child, will be a prophet of the Most High God. You will go before the Lord and make people ready to hear him."

When John grew up, he lived in the desert. He stayed there until God called him to preach a special message to the people. God made him to be a great prophet. He was known as John the Baptist. His purpose was to prepare the people to receive the coming Savior.

THE BIRTH OF JESUS
MATTHEW 1:18-25
LUKE 2:1-7

Soon after John the Baptist was born, Joseph, the man who was engaged to Mary, found out that she was pregnant. Because they had not had been together sexually, he no longer wanted to marry her, but he also did not want to disgrace Mary publicly. Instead, he thought to end the relationship quietly and move on with his life.

As he thought about this an angel of the Lord appeared to him in a dream and said: "Joseph, God does not want you to be ashamed of Mary. Rather, he wants you to take her to be your wife. The child growing in her womb was conceived by the Holy Spirit. He is God's very own Son. When he is born you are to name him Jesus because he will save God's people from their sins. And God wants you to take care of him as his earthly father until he grows up."

When Joseph woke up from his dream, he realized that this baby was the one who the Bible had predicted would come to be the Savior of the world.

So he did exactly what the angel told him and took Mary to be his wife.

After they were married they settled in Nazareth. Then a command came from the great Roman emperor Caesar Augustus. Although Herod was the king in Israel, Augustus was the ruler of many countries. All the kings had to obey his orders. Caesar Augustus ordered each family to go to the husband's hometown because the emperor wanted to count all the people under his rule. Because Joseph was from Bethlehem, he and Mary had to travel from Nazareth to Bethlehem to put their name on the emperor's list.

It was a difficult journey, especially for Mary. They had to walk down the mountains around Nazareth to the river Jordan and follow the river almost to its end before climbing up the mountains around Bethlehem. When Joseph and Mary arrived, they found that Bethlehem was filled with people who had come to put their names on the list. All the rooms were taken. There was no place for them to stay.

The only shelter Joseph could find was a stable where the cows were kept. That night Mary started to feel the pains of childbirth, and Jesus was born there in that stable. They found a manger, a feeding trough for the cows, and after filling it with straw they laid the baby Jesus in it. So Jesus spent his first night on earth in a manger in Bethlehem.

The Shepherds & the Old Man

Luke 2:8-35

On the very night Jesus was born in a stable in Bethlehem, some shepherds were tending their sheep in a nearby field. It was very dark when suddenly a great light blazed around them. When they looked up they saw that an angel of the Lord stood before them. As they gazed at the glorious light radiating from the angel, they felt great fear in their hearts.

The angel said to them: "Do not be afraid. I bring you good news that will bring great joy for you and all the people. Today in the little town of Bethlehem, a Savior has been born to you. He is Christ the Lord."

As soon as he said this, the shepherds looked up and saw that the dark sky around them lit up with thousands of angels. They were all singing, "Glory to God in the highest. And peace on earth to all whom God is well pleased."

Then just as suddenly as the angels arrived, they disappeared into the darkness. The shepherds were stunned and asked each other, "What just happened?"

After they collected their thoughts they said to each other, "What should we do? Let's go to Bethlehem and see this thing that the angel told us about."

So they quickly ran to the town and found Joseph, his young wife, and the little baby Jesus lying in the manger. They told Mary and Joseph about the glorious angel and all they had seen out in the field. After the shepherds returned to their sheep,

Mary treasured their words in her heart for a long time. She remembered how the angel had visited her to tell her that she would give birth to God's Son. And now the thought of thousands of angels announcing this birth to the world was just too much for her to understand all at once. It made her realize how great God was and how great was this baby that she had just borne.

Eight days later, Joseph and Mary officially named the child *Jesus*, the very name the angel had said that he should be given. The name *Jesus* means "salvation," and Jesus was born to bring salvation to the world.

When Jesus was forty days old, Joseph and Mary brought him to the temple in Jerusalem to give an offering to show that Jesus belonged to the Lord. At that moment, the Spirit of the Lord told an old man named Simeon to go up to them. Many years before, when Simeon was a young man, the Lord had promised Simeon that he would not die until he had seen with his own eyes the promised Savior. Now after many, many years of waiting, that time had come.

The Spirit said to Simeon, "This little one is the promised Christ." Then Simeon took the baby in his arms and said, "Now, O Lord, let your servant depart in peace; for my eyes have seen your salvation."

Then Simeon blessed the child and said to Mary: "This child will expose what is bad in people's hearts. And because of that, many will hate him. And their hatred will cause you great pain." He was referring to the time when Mary would see her Son nailed to the cross.

THE STAR & THE WISE MEN
MATTHEW 2:1-23

The little baby Jesus stayed in the stable in Bethlehem for only a few days. Then Joseph and Mary found a room in a house. This is where strange men visited Jesus from a land far away.

These men studied the stars. One night they saw an unusual star shining in the sky. They knew the appearance of this star signaled that a powerful new king would soon be born in the land of Israel. These men felt called by God to visit this newborn king to pay their respect. After a very long journey from the East, through many countries, with camels and horses, they came to Jerusalem, a few miles away from Bethlehem. They thought everyone would know about this newborn king and could tell them where he might be found. So they asked, "Where is he who is born to be King of the Jews? We have seen his star in the East and have come to worship him."

But no one knew what they were talking about. News of their visit reached King Herod. Herod was a wicked man, and when he heard that someone was born to be king, he became suspicious and jealous. He feared that this new king would overthrow him and take his power. So he made up his mind to kill the baby king.

First, he had to find him. So he sent for scholars who had studied the books of the Old Testament and asked them what they knew about this king that the wise men were seeking. He asked, "Where is this new King of Israel supposed to be born?" They looked at the writings of the prophets and said, "He is to be born in Bethlehem. For it is written, 'And you, Bethlehem . . . out of you shall come one who will rule my people Israel.'"

So Herod sent for the wise men to meet them privately. He tried to make them believe that he, too, wanted to honor the new king. "Go to Bethlehem and search carefully for the little child. When you find him, bring word to me so that I, too, may go and worship him."

The wise men left Herod, continued on their journey, and followed the star until it led them to the very house in Bethlehem where the little child was. They came in and saw the baby with Mary, his mother. They knew at once that this was the king, and they fell down on their faces and worshiped him as Lord. Then they brought out gifts of gold and precious perfumes called frankincense and myrrh, and they gave them to the child Jesus.

That night God spoke to the wise men in a dream telling them not to report back to Herod. So they left without telling Herod anything and returned to their own land.

Then an angel of God warned Joseph in a dream, "Herod will try to kill this child. Take the little child and his mother, and go quickly down to Egypt." At once Joseph rose up in the night, took his wife and the baby, and quickly fled to Egypt.

When Herod learned that the wise men had gone home without bringing him any word, he was furious. He immediately sent soldiers to Bethlehem and commanded them to kill all the little boys in Bethlehem who were two years old and younger. All the mothers of Bethlehem screamed out in howls of despair as their children were taken from them and murdered!

Soon after this awful event, cruel King Herod died. Then the angel of the Lord came again to Joseph in a dream and said to him, "Herod is dead. You may now take the child back to Israel."

So Joseph took Mary and Jesus back to Nazareth, the town where they had lived before Jesus was born. So Jesus grew up in Nazareth. There Mary gave birth to other sons and daughters who would become Jesus' brothers and sisters.

"Behold, the days are coming," says the LORD,

"That I will raise to David a Branch of righteousness;

A King shall reign and prosper,

And execute judgment and righteousness in the earth.

JEREMIAH 23:5

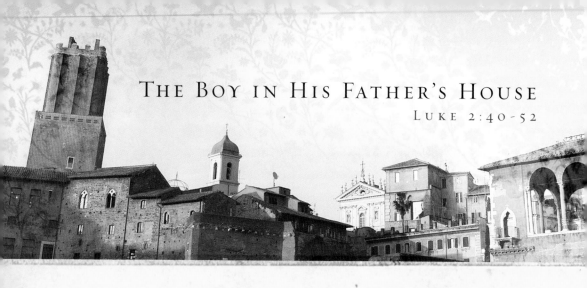

THE BOY IN HIS FATHER'S HOUSE

LUKE 2:40-52

Jesus was about three years old when he came from Egypt to live in Nazareth. He lived there as a boy and as a young man.

The Bible tells us very little about his growing up. Because Joseph was a carpenter, the family probably didn't have much money. It is likely that they lived in a one-room house with a dirt floor and a hole in the wall for a window. They would eat their meals sitting on the floor and sleep on mats that were rolled up during the daytime.

Jesus would have learned to read at the Jewish place of worship called the synagogue. As a child, he would go with Joseph to the synagogue twice each week. They would sit and hear the Old Testament of the Bible read and explained. Jesus was taught to memorize many long parts of the Bible by heart.

Once a year during the spring, Jews from all over Israel would go to the great city of Jerusalem to worship during a feast called Passover. This holiday was a celebration to help them remember how God had rescued the Jewish people from the Egyptians and brought them to the land of Israel.

When Jesus was twelve years old, he went with his family to Jerusalem to celebrate the Passover at the great temple of the Lord. His heart was stirred as he walked through the courts of the temple and saw the priests in their white robes. Even as a boy, Jesus knew that he was God's Son. He also knew that this temple was his Father's house.

As he listened to the teachers preach about God, his mind became so filled with thoughts that when it was time to go home to Nazareth, he stayed behind.

Now in those days people from the same town traveled together in large groups. So at first Joseph and Mary thought he was with them, traveling in another part of the group. But soon they became very worried because no one knew where Jesus was.

Joseph and Mary hurried back to Jerusalem to find him. They looked everywhere for him. They asked friends and relatives if they had seen him. But no one knew where he was. After several days of looking they went up to the temple with heavy hearts. To their surprise they found him sitting with the teachers, listening to the lessons from the Bible, and asking them many questions. Everyone was amazed at how deeply he thought about these things and how vast his knowledge was about God.

His mother spoke to him sharply. "Son," she said. "Why didn't you tell us where you were? Didn't you know that your father and I were worried sick about you?"

Jesus answered, "Didn't you know that I would be in my Father's house?"

Mary realized that Jesus had called God his very own father. And although Jesus loved Joseph, Jesus knew that Joseph was not his real father. Mary remembered this for the rest of her life.

Jesus then returned to Nazareth with Mary and Joseph and obeyed them as his parents. He continued to grow in wisdom and was respected by all, for there was something about him that attracted everyone to him.

Jesus learned to be a carpenter. When Joseph died, Jesus, as the oldest son, took over the care of the family. He worked in a carpentry shop and lived a simple and quiet life in the country village of Nazareth until he was thirty years of age.

He shall cry to Me, 'You are my Father,
My God, and the rock of my salvation.'
Also I will make him My firstborn,
The highest of the kings of the earth.

PSALM 89:26-27

THE PROPHET IN THE WILDERNESS

MATTHEW 3:1-17; LUKE 3:1-22
MARK 1:1-11; JOHN 1:19-28

It had been more than four hundred years since God had last sent a prophet to speak to his people. A prophet is someone to whom God speaks directly, not someone who learns only from studying the Bible. And now after all these many years, news that God had sent a new prophet was spreading fast.

His name was John, the son of Zechariah and Elizabeth, Mary's cousin. Mary had visited Elizabeth when she was pregnant with John and just after God had told Mary that she was to give birth to Jesus. That happened thirty years earlier.

John lived in the desert, where he could be alone and could listen to the voice of God without any distractions. Because he spoke the words God had given to him, people from all over Israel went out into the desert across the Jordan River to hear John preach.

John dressed simply with clothes made of camel's hair and a leather belt around his waist. He ate dried locusts with a bit of wild honey.

This was the message that he preached: "Turn away from your selfish living and do what is right. God will send his promised Messiah to judge you and prepare you to live in his eternal Kingdom."

Some people were frightened by this message and asked John, "What must we do to be ready for God's kingdom?"

John told them directly: "Share the blessings God has given to you with those who have less. If you have two coats, give one to him who has none. If you have more food than you need, give to him who is hungry."

The tax collectors, who often cheated people by forcing them to pay more taxes than they owed and then keeping the extra money for themselves, also came to him. They felt guilty about what they had done, and they asked John, "What should we do?" John said to them, "Collect only tax money you are allowed."

When the religious leaders came to him, John was most harsh with them. These men tried to impress people by their long public prayers and their gifts to the poor. But in their hearts they cared little about prayer or the poor. They cared only for themselves. John said to them, "You are the most wicked of all! What makes you think that you are fooling God with your false religion?"

John's preaching showed the people how far away from God they really were. Many felt very sorry in their hearts for the sins they had committed. They asked God to forgive them and to help them live their lives in the way God wanted them to.

Those who truly wanted to change their lives were baptized by John in the Jordan River. Baptism was God's way of showing the people that He had forgiven them and had washed away their sins from their souls. Because John baptized so many people he became known as "John the Baptist."

But John knew that the baptism he offered was not enough. People would sin again. They needed something more powerful to save them—a power that only God could give.

So John always preached these words pointing beyond himself: "I baptize you with water, but the one who comes after me is greater than me. I am not even worthy to untie his sandals. I baptize you with water, but he will baptize you with the Holy Spirit who will give you power to fight sin and do God's work.

Jesus was thirty years old when he went to be baptized by John. When John saw Jesus coming to him to be baptized, he knew that this was the Messiah that God had promised. John said to Jesus, "You want me to baptize you? I need you to baptize me!"

But Jesus said to him, "No. It is God's plan that I be baptized by you."

So John baptized Jesus just as he had baptized everyone else. When Jesus came up out of the water, John saw the Holy Spirit come down on Jesus like a dove. And a voice came from heaven, saying, "This is my Son, whom I love. With him I am well pleased."

The voice of one crying in the wilderness:

"Prepare the way of the LORD;

Make straight in the desert

A highway for our God."

ISAIAH 40:3

Jesus in the Desert

MARK 1:12-15; LUKE 4:1-15

From early childhood Jesus knew that God had a special plan for him. God's purpose was confirmed at his baptism. As soon as Jesus came out of the water, he heard the voice from heaven say, "You are my Son, whom I love; with you I am well pleased."

God wanted the world to know who Jesus was, where he came from, and what authority he had. It also signaled from that point forward God, through his Holy Spirit, would direct Jesus completely to do the work he was sent to do—to rescue his people from the power of sin.

Immediately after Jesus was baptized, the Spirit of God sent him into the desert to be alone with God. While in the desert, he was so absorbed in his time with God that he went without food for forty days and nights. When the forty days were over, Jesus was starving and desperately weak. It was at this moment, when Jesus was most weak, that Satan came and tried to tempt him from doing the work God had sent him to do.

"If you are the Son of God," challenged Satan, "why don't you command that these stones be changed into bread? Then you won't be so hungry."

Jesus knew that he could do this. But he also knew that he mustn't give in to the devil's temptation. That would be too easy and would allow Satan to manipulate him. This would undermine the work God wanted him to do. He knew he must resist the devil. So he said to Satan: "It is written in God's book, 'Man shall not live

28 THE JOURNEY OF JESUS

by bread alone, but by every word that comes from the mouth of God.'"

Then Satan led Jesus to Jerusalem, the holy city, and brought him to the top of the highest tower on the temple of God. The devil said to him, "You could show off how great you are by falling down to the ground from here. Everyone would be impressed because, as you know, it is written in the Bible, 'God will send his angels to protect you; so that you will not even hurt your foot when you land against the stones.'"

But Jesus resisted and said, "'Thou shall not tempt the LORD thy God.'"

Satan was not yet finished. He had one more great temptation in mind to stop Jesus from carrying out God's plans. Satan took him up a very high mountain where he could see all the great cities and kingdoms of the world. They all looked so beautiful in their splendor. He said to Jesus, "All these great kingdoms are under my control. I will give them all to you if you will fall on your knees and worship me instead of God."

Jesus became angry and said, "Get away from me, Satan! It is written, 'You shall worship the LORD your God, and serve him alone.'"

Then the devil left him for a time. He would return later and have his way with Jesus when the earthly rulers would conspire against Jesus and have him sent to the cross.

After resisting Satan, the angels came and gave Jesus food to eat. Then he returned to the river Jordan where he had been baptized. There John the Baptist saw Jesus coming toward him, and he said, "Behold the Lamb of God, who takes away the sin of the world! This is the Son of God"

Jesus was now ready to begin his work.

THE FIRST FIVE FOLLOWERS OF JESUS

JOHN 1:29-51
MATTHEW 4:18-22
MARK 1:16-20

The next morning, John the Baptist was standing with two young fishermen who had come from the Sea of Galilee. One was named Andrew and the other John. When they heard John call Jesus, "the Lamb of God," they followed Jesus.

Jesus turned around and asked, "Why are you following me?"

They replied, "Master, where do you live?"

"Come and see," said Jesus.

They followed Jesus and spent the rest of the day with him. Andrew and John were the first, after John the Baptist, to believe that Jesus was the Savior God had promised.

Andrew had a brother named Simon who was also a fisherman. Andrew went to look for him. When he found him he said, "Simon, we have found the Messiah, the Christ, who is to be the King of Israel."

Before Andrew introduced Simon to him, Jesus said, "Your name is Simon, the son of Jonah. But I will give you a new name. You shall be called *Peter*, which means 'the Rock.'" So from that day on he was called Simon Peter, that is, "Simon the Rock." Jesus now had three followers.

The next day Jesus met a man named Philip, also from Galilee. He said to Philip, "Follow me."

Philip was Jesus' fourth disciple. Philip had a friend named Nathaniel. Philip said to him, "We have found the one of whom Moses and the prophets wrote about in the Bible, the Messiah, the Christ! He is Jesus of Nazareth."

"Nazareth!" Nathaniel said with surprise. "How can anything good come from there?"

Philip said, "Come and see."

As soon as Jesus saw Nathaniel he said, "Here is a true man of Israel, one who speaks what he thinks."

Nathaniel was surprised to hear Jesus say this. He asked, "Teacher, how do you know anything about me?"

Jesus said, "Even before Philip called you, I saw you standing under the fig tree."

Nathaniel was even more surprised and said, "Teacher, you must be the Son of God! You must be the King of Israel!"

Jesus said, "You believe in me just because I said that I saw you under the fig tree? You will see things much greater than this. You will see heaven opened and the angels of God going up and down to heaven through me."

Andrew, John, Simon Peter, Philip, and Nathaniel were the first five people to become followers of Jesus. They were called "disciples."

Good and upright is the LORD;

Therefore He teaches sinners in the way.

The humble He guides in justice,

And the humble He teaches His way.

PSALM 25:8-9

Jesus' First Miracle

A few days after Jesus met his first followers they all went to a very large wedding in Cana, a town near Jesus' hometown of Nazareth. Jesus' mother, Mary, was also at this wedding.

After the wedding there was a great feast, and after several hours all the wine was gone. There was no more to drink. Mary looked at Jesus and wanted him to help. She said to him, "They have no wine."

Jesus seemed surprised at his mother's request. He said to her, "What does this have to do with me? The time to reveal my power has not yet come."

But his mother was persistent and said to the servants, "Do whatever he tells you to do."

Nearby stood six large stone jars, each as large as a barrel that could hold up to thirty gallons of water. These jars were empty because the guests had used the water to wash their hands and feet as they came in from walking to the wedding. Jesus said to the servants, "Fill those jars with water."

The servants filled the jars up to the very top. Then Jesus said to them, "Pour out what you need from the jars and take it to the master of the feast."

When they poured out the water, they saw that it had been turned into wine. The master did not know where this wine came from. He assumed it came from the bridegroom. So he went over to the young man who had just been married and said to him happily, "Most people bring out the best wine first, but you have kept the best wine for last."

This was the first time that Jesus used the miraculous power God had given him. He used this power for good and to show that he was the son of God. When his followers saw this miracle, their faith in Jesus grew stronger than it was before.

And the Spirit and the bride say, "Come!" And let him who hears say, "Come!"
And let him who thirsts come. Whoever desires, let him take the water of life freely.

REVELATION 22:17

The Samaritan Woman
by the Well

Jesus left Jerusalem with his disciples and went toward Galilee. To get there he had to pass through Samaria, where the Samaritans lived. Both the Samaritans and the Jews worshiped the God of the Bible, but the Samaritans only read from the first five books of the Bible. They did not believe that the other books were really from God, and they had their own temple and their own priests.

Jews and Samaritans despised each other. They never worshiped together or even spoke to each other. So when Jews traveled to Galilee, they would go all the way around Samaria to avoid contact with Samaritans rather than take the shorter journey through the region.

But Jesus decided to walk straight through Samaria. He stopped by an old well near a little village called Sychar at the foot of a mountain called Mount Gerazim. This well had been dug seventeen hundred years before by Jacob, one of the most important people in the Bible.

By the time Jesus arrived at Jacob's well, he had walked many miles and was hungry. His disciples went into a nearby village to buy food. Jesus was also very thirsty. He looked down the well and saw soothing water to drink, but he had no rope or jar to draw the water up from the well.

36 THE JOURNEY OF JESUS

At that moment a Samaritan woman came to the well. She had a water jar on her shoulder and a rope in her hand. Even though Jews do not speak to Samaritans, Jesus asked her, "Please give me a drink."

The woman could tell he was a Jew. She said, "How dare you ask me for a drink?"

But Jesus knew what was in her heart. He had compassion on her and said, "If you knew who it is that asks you for a drink and what he has to give, you would ask him to give you living water."

She thought to herself before she asked, "What is this living water? where do you get it? Do you think that you are greater than our father Jacob who drank from this well?"

Jesus answered: "Everyone who drinks water from this well will be thirsty again. But whoever drinks the water I give will never thirst again. The water I give is a spring of water that always flows. It even gives eternal life."

The woman was moved in her heart. "Sir," she said. "Please give me this water to drink, so I will never be thirsty again."

Jesus told her, "First, go home and call your husband and bring him here."

"I have no husband," she replied.

"Yes, I know you have no husband," said Jesus. "You have already had five husbands. And the man you are now living with is not your husband."

The woman was startled by this. She tried to change the subject. "I can see that you are a prophet. We Samaritans worship God here. But you Jews say that the only place to worship God is in Jerusalem. So which is really the right place to worship God?"

Jesus said, "Believe me, woman, a time is coming when you will not worship God here or in Jerusalem. You Samaritans do not know what the Jews know. Salvation comes from the Jews." Jesus told her this to let her know that all of the Old Testament, even the parts that the Samaritans did not accept, is true and reveals God's plan. "There is a time coming when the true believers of God will worship Him wherever they are in spirit and truth. These are the kind of worshipers God wants. Because God is spirit, it must be that his worshipers will worship Him in spirit and in truth."

The woman said, "I know that the Messiah will be coming soon. When he comes, he will explain everything to us."

Then Jesus declared, "I am the Messiah."

The woman was so startled by what Jesus said that she left her water jar, ran back to her village, and said to the people, "Come, see a man who told me everything that I have done in all my life! Could he be the Messiah we are waiting for?"

When the woman came back she brought many Samaritans with her. They urged him to stay with them. He stayed two days, and many more Samaritans believed in Jesus. They said to the woman, "We no longer believe just from what you said; now we have heard him ourselves, and we know that this man really is the Savior of the world."

For I know that my Redeemer lives,

And He shall stand at last on the earth.

JOB 19:25

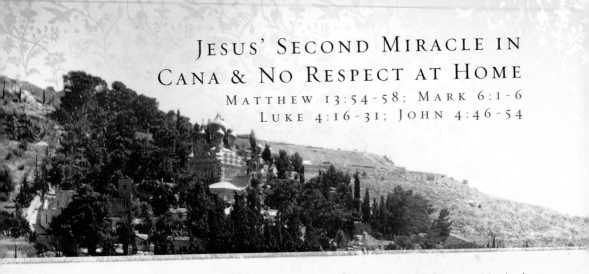

JESUS' SECOND MIRACLE IN CANA & NO RESPECT AT HOME

MATTHEW 13:54-58; MARK 6:1-6
LUKE 4:16-31; JOHN 4:46-54

After Jesus traveled through Samaria he came to Cana, the place where he had performed his first miracle by turning water into wine. News that Jesus had returned spread quickly, and a large crowd came to him.

One who sought Jesus was a high-ranking official from Herod's royal palace. He came all the way from Capernaum to beg Jesus to heal his son who was dying from sickness.

Jesus said to the man, "Do you believe in me only because you see miraculous signs and wonders?

The man replied, "Sir, come before my child dies."

Jesus answered, "Go, your son will live."

When he arrived at home a servant ran to meet him. "Your son is well!" he said.

The man asked, "At what time did the fever leave my son?"

"Yesterday at one o'clock in the afternoon," the servant said.

The father knew that was the time that Jesus told him, "Your son will live." He was amazed, and he and everyone else in his household believed.

This was Jesus' second miracle.

Jesus then decided to go to Nazareth, his hometown. This is where he grew up and where his mother, brothers, and sisters still lived. Everyone in the town knew him. Jesus knew it was time to tell them who he really was and what God had sent him to do.

On the Sabbath he went into the same synagogue where he worshiped God as a child. The people had heard that Jesus, whom they knew as a carpenter, now had a reputation as a great teacher. The synagogue was filled to capacity.

Jesus stood up to read from the Scriptures. The minister handed him a scroll that contained writings from Isaiah the prophet. Jesus turned to the sixty-first chapter and read:

> "The Spirit of the LORD is upon me, He has anointed me to preach good news to the poor. He has sent me to proclaim freedom to prisoners and to give sight to the blind, to free those who who have been oppressed and to proclaim God's grace to men."

When Jesus had finished reading, he rolled up the scroll and gave it back to the minister. Then he said, "Today as you heard it read, this scripture has been fulfilled."

Everyone's eyes were fixed on him and many were impressed by his teaching and many spoke well of him. They had heard of the miracles he had performed in Cana, and they wanted him to do something spectacular like that in his hometown. When he wouldn't perform a miracle on command, some in the crowd began to challenge him.

"Where did this man get this teaching?" they asked. "Isn't he only a carpenter? How dare he try to teach us?" And they were offended by him.

Jesus said to them, "Only in his hometown, among his relatives, and in his own house, is a prophet without honor."

All this made the people angry. They grabbed Jesus and took him up to the top of the hill above the city where they wanted to throw him down to his death.

But Jesus, knowing that his time to die had not yet come, turned around, walked straight through the middle of the crowd, and left Nazareth for Capernaum.

The Leper & the Man Let Down Through the Roof

Mark 1:29-2:12
Matthew 8:14-15, 9:1-8
Luke 4:38-44, 5:12-26

After a day of healing and teaching great crowds of people in Capernaum, Jesus lay down to rest in the house of Simon Peter. But very early the next morning, while it was still dark, he got up and went out of the house to a place where he could be alone with God. There he prayed for a long time.

When Simon and the other disciples got up they began to look for him. When they found him they said, "Everybody is looking for you!"

But Jesus said, "Let us go to other towns and villages where I must also preach about the kingdom of God. This is why God sent me."

So Jesus went through all the towns in Galilee, preaching the good news of the kingdom, healing every kind of sickness and disease, and driving out evil spirits. And great crowds followed him wherever he went.

While he was on this journey, a man with leprosy, a terrible skin disease that no one could cure, came to him. This man fell at Jesus' feet and cried out, "Lord, if you are willing, you can cure my leprosy!"

Jesus, filled with compassion, reached out his hand and touched the man with leprosy. "I am willing," he said. "Be clean!" Immediately the leprosy left him, and the man's skin was absolutely pure and clean.

Jesus said to him, "Don't tell anyone about this, but go to the temple and give an offering according to what the law of God commands you must do after such a healing. And make sure that the priests see that you have been completely cured."

Jesus told him not to tell anyone else about this because he knew that if the miracle were made known that even larger crowds would come to him for healing and would prevent him from preaching about the Kingdom of God, the very thing God had sent him to do.

But the man with leprosy went out and told everyone that Jesus had healed him. And just as Jesus had known, great crowds came to him from all the towns and villages. He had to hide out in the countryside to be by himself. Still, the people came to him from everywhere.

After a time Jesus came back to Capernaum. As soon as the people heard that he had returned, a great crowd came to see him. They filled a house where he was teaching, and the crowds even spilled over into the streets around it.

In the crowd listening to Jesus were not only those who admired him, but some who hated him. They were religious teachers whose hearts were not right with God. They were jealous of Jesus and the power of his teaching. These men came to try to find ways to turn the people away from Jesus.

While Jesus was teaching, and these men were listening, the roof of the house was suddenly taken away above them. They looked up and saw that four men had dug through the thatched roof so that they could lower a crippled man who was lying on a mat into the house. This man was helpless. He could neither stand nor walk. He so wanted to come to Jesus, and his friends were so sure that Jesus could heal him and make him well. When Jesus saw their faith in him, he said to the man, "Son, your sins are forgiven!"

The enemies of Jesus heard these words and whispered to themselves, "This man is telling lies! He says he can forgive sins. But we know that only God has the power to forgive sins."

Jesus knew their thoughts so he said, "Why do you think evil in your hearts about me? Which is the easier to say to the crippled man? 'Your sins are forgiven,' or to say, 'Get up and walk'? But that you may know that I have the power to forgive sins . . ." He said to the crippled man, "Get up, take your mat, and walk."

At once the crippled man's feet and legs became strong. He stood up, rolled up the mat he was lying on, and walked out in front of the whole crowd. This amazed everyone, and they praised God saying, "We have never seen anything like this."

In this way Jesus showed everyone that he had the power to forgive sins.

Jesus Chooses His Twelve Disciples

Mark 2:13-17, 3:13-19
Matthew 9:9-13, 10:1-4
Luke 5:27-32, 6:12-16

The Romans hired a few Jewish men to collect taxes for them. They were tough men who forced some Jews to pay more tax money than they actually owed so that they could keep the extra money for themselves. Some did not do this, but the Jews hated all the tax collectors just the same.

One day as Jesus was teaching a large crowd, he saw a tax collector named Levi who also was called Matthew. It was common for Jews to have two names. He was sitting at a table counting tax money when he heard Jesus say, "Follow me."

Matthew felt compelled to leave the money behind and follow Jesus. The people couldn't believe that Jesus would ask a despised tax collector to be one of his disciples. Others wondered how Matthew would get along with men like Peter, James, and John who ordinarily would hate people like him.

But Jesus had a plan for Matthew. He wanted Matthew to write down all that Jesus said and did so that after he was crucified and resurrected, people would know about his life on earth. It was this Matthew, the hated tax collector, who wrote the Gospel of Matthew.

One day, not long after Jesus called him, Matthew had a dinner in honor of Jesus at his home. Matthew invited many tax collectors and other men who were considered wicked because of the way they lived. But Jesus didn't mind being around people who others hated. That is why he came. When the Pharisees saw Jesus conversing with these people, they thought that Jesus was approving of the way they lived. They asked his disciples, "Why does he eat and talk with tax collectors and sinners?"

They didn't realize that the way to change men's hearts was to get know them and show that you care for them. So when Jesus heard people question what he was doing, he said: "When do you call a doctor? When you are well or sick? You call a doctor when you are sick. I did not come to call righteous people, but sinners who need to be made well."

A few days later, Jesus went up a mountain to be alone with God. He stayed there all night. When he came down, he called to him those who he wanted to follow him more closely. He chose twelve men to live with him all the time so that he could teach them God's ways very carefully and then send them out with power to preach, to drive out demons, and to heal the sick.

These are the names of the twelve he appointed: Simon (to whom he gave the name Peter); James son of Zebedee and his brother, John; Andrew, Philip, Bartholomew, Matthew, Thomas, James son of Alphaeus, Thaddaeus, Simon the Zealot, and Judas Iscariot, who betrayed him.

Peter was the leader among them. The Gospel of Mark is really the stories Peter preached about Jesus in his later years. Peter had a follower named Mark who wrote them down for him. That is why Mark's name is attached to that gospel. John wrote the Gospel of John. Later on, a man named Luke would join them and write the Gospel of Luke.

And He shall stand and feed His flock
In the strength of the LORD,
In the majesty of the name of the LORD His God;
And they shall abide,
For now He shall be great
To the ends of the earth;

MICAH 5:4

I will raise up for them a Prophet like you from among their brethren, and will put My words in His mouth, and He shall speak to them all that I command Him.

DEUTERONOMY 18:18

THE TEACHINGS OF JESUS
MATTHEW 4:23-7:29

Jesus traveled throughout Galilee, and people brought to him sick and tormented people, those who were possessed by devils, lunatics, and the paralyzed. And he healed them.

One day as a large crowd followed him, he went up on a mountainside and sat down. His disciples came to him, and he began to teach them. Matthew wrote down the words he spoke. This part of the Gospel of Matthew is called the Sermon on the Mount, and it begins like this:

> Blessed are the poor in spirit, for theirs is the kingdom of heaven.
>
> Blessed are they that mourn, for they shall be comforted.
>
> Blessed are the meek, for they shall inherit the earth.

Blessed are they that hunger and thirst for righteousness, for they shall be filled.

Blessed are the merciful, for they shall receive mercy.

Blessed are the pure in heart, for they shall see God.

Blessed are the peacemakers, for they shall be called children of God.

Blessed are they who are persecuted for righteousness' sake, for theirs is the kingdom of heaven.

Jesus also taught these things:

"You are the light of the world. A city on a hill cannot be hidden. Neither do people light a candle and put it under a bowl. Instead they put it on its candlestick, so that it gives light to everyone in the house. In the same way, let your light shine before men, that they may see the good deeds you do on behalf of God and give praise to your Father in heaven. . . .

"Do not store up for yourselves treasures on earth, where moth and rust destroy, and where thieves break in and steal. But store up for yourselves treasures in heaven, where moth and rust do not destroy, and where thieves do not break in and steal. For where your treasure is, there your heart will be also. . . .

"Do not be worried about the things in your life such as what shall we eat, or what shall we drink; nor for your body, what you shall wear. Is not the life more than food, and the body more than clothing? For your heavenly Father knows your needs. But seek first his kingdom and his righteousness, and all these things will be given to you as well."

This is what Jesus taught his disciples about prayer:

"And when you pray, keep it simple. Many people think they will be heard because they use many words. Do not be like that, for your Father knows what you need before you ask him. This is how you should pray:

> Our Father who is in heaven, Holy is your name.
>
> Your kingdom come. Your will be done on earth, as it is in heaven.
>
> Give us this day our daily bread.
>
> And forgive us our sins, as we forgive those who sin against us.
>
> Lead us not into temptation, but deliver us from evil,
>
> For you are the kingdom, and the power, and the glory,
> forever. Amen.

"For when you forgive people when they sin against you, your heavenly Father will also forgive you. But if you do not forgive people their sins, your Father will not forgive your sins. . . .

"Ask God, and it shall be given to you; seek God, and you shall find him; knock on his door, and he shall open it for you and let you in. For the one who asks will receive; and the one who seeks him will find him; and the one who knocks on His door will see the door opened for him."

And this is how Jesus ended his sermon:

"Everyone who hears these teachings of mine and puts them into practice is like a wise person who built his house on the rock. The rain came down, the streams rose, and the winds blew and beat against that house; yet it did not fall, because it had its foundation on the rock. But everyone who hears these teachings of mine and does not put them into practice is like a foolish man who built his house on sand. The rain came down, the streams rose, and the winds blew and beat against that house, and it fell with a great crash."

When Jesus had finished teaching, the crowds were amazed at his words because he spoke with so much power. His teaching was unlike any teaching they had heard before. Their regular teachers had no power to change people's hearts.

The Centurion's Faith
& A Dead Boy Raised to Life

LUKE 7:1-17
MATTHEW 8:5-13

After Jesus had finished preaching the Sermon on the Mount, he returned to Capernaum. When he arrived some of the leaders in that town told him about a Roman centurion (an officer in charge of a hundred soldiers) who had a servant whom he loved very much who was ill and near death. This centurion was special to the Jews because he respected them and their religion. He even took his own money and built the synagogue in that town.

The centurion asked some of the Jewish leaders to speak to Jesus and ask him to come and heal his servant. When they saw Jesus they pleaded with him and said, "This man deserves to have you do this, because he loves our nation and has built our synagogue." So Jesus went with them.

But as he approached the centurion's house, the centurion sent a messenger to Jesus. "Lord, I do not deserve to have you come to my house. That is why I asked others to speak to you for me. I do not consider myself worthy to come to you on my own. But I want you to know that I believe in you and know that you have the power to heal my servant. Just say the word and my servant will be healed. For I understand authority. When I give an order to a soldier to go, he goes. If I tell him to come, he comes. And if I say to my servant, 'do this,' he does it."

When Jesus heard this, he was amazed at the faith of the centurion. He turned to the crowd and said, "I tell you the truth, I have not found such great faith in all of Israel." Then Jesus told the messengers to go back to the centurion's house. When they returned they found that the servant had been healed.

Jesus was beginning to show that he had come not only to save Jewish people, but also all the people in the world who would believe in him.

The next day Jesus left Capernaum and came to a town called Nain. His disciples and a large crowd traveled with him. When they arrived they saw a crowd of people following the body of a dead boy being carried out for burial. The boy was the only son of a widow. She was now all alone. When Jesus saw the mother's tears and how much pain she was in, his heart went out to her. He said to her, "Don't cry."

Then Jesus went up to the coffin and touched it. Those carrying the coffin stopped. Then Jesus said, "Young man, I say to you, get up!"

At that moment the young man sat up and began to talk. Then Jesus gave the boy who was dead but now alive again back to his mother.

The people were shocked by this wonderful miracle they had just seen. They said, "God has sent to us a great prophet to help his people!"

News that Jesus had raised a dead boy to life spread very quickly throughout the whole area.

THE WOMAN WHO LOVED JESUS

While Jesus was preaching through Galilee, a Pharisee named Simon invited Jesus to dine with him at his home. Simon did not believe in Jesus. He invited him over to see if he could find something wrong with Jesus' teaching or behavior. When Jesus arrived, Simon did not welcome him or show him respect. He did not bring water to wash Jesus' feet. In those days people walked long distances in open sandals. Their feet would get very dirty. When a visitor came to your house it was a sign of welcome and respect to wash the visitor's feet, but Simon did not do that for Jesus.

In those days they ate their meals differently than how we do today. Instead of sitting in chairs around a table, they would lie on their stomachs on floor beds with their heads and arms toward the food and their bare feet exposed at the other end of the bed. From this position they could reach out and take the food to eat it.

While Jesus was eating, a woman came into the room. She brought with her a beautiful jar filled with very expensive perfume. She came to the end of the bed where Jesus lay and began to wash his feet with her tears. Then she wiped them dry with her long hair. After she had done this, she kissed Jesus' feet and poured the expensive perfume on them.

When Simon saw this, he thought to himself, "If this Jesus was really a prophet sent by God, he would know that this woman is a prostitute. He would not have let her touch him."

Jesus knew this woman came to show him that she was truly sorry for her sins. She was asking Jesus to forgive her and to give her the power to live the life God wanted her to live.

Jesus also knew what Simon was thinking. So he asked Simon a question: "Two men owed money to the same moneylender. One of them owed five hundred denarii." (One denarius was what a man would pay his workers for a one full day of work. So borrowing five hundred denarii was like owing seventeen months of pay.) "The other man owed him only fifty. Neither of them had the money to pay him back, so the moneylender canceled the debts of both men. Now which of these two men do you think will love the moneylender more?"

"I suppose the one who had the most money forgiven would love the moneylender more," said Simon.

"Yes," Jesus said. Then he turned toward the woman and said to Simon: "When I came into your house, you did not give me any water for my feet. But this woman wet my feet with her tears and wiped them with her hair. You gave me no kiss, but this woman has not stopped kissing my feet. You did not anoint my head with oil, but she has poured perfume on my feet.

"You acted as if you owed me nothing and you showed me no love or respect. She knew how much she owed me and loved me greatly. Therefore, Simon, I say to you, her sins, which are many, are forgiven."

Then Jesus said directly to the woman, "Your sins are forgiven."

Those who were around the table with Simon were surprised at Jesus' words and whispered to each other, "Who is this man who thinks he has the power to forgive sins?"

But Jesus said to the woman, "Your faith has saved you; go in peace!"

Indeed the LORD has proclaimed

To the end of the world:

"Say to the daughter of Zion,

'Surely your salvation is coming;

Behold, His reward is with Him,

And His work before Him.' "

ISAIAH 62:11

THE WILD MAN & THE PIGS

MARK 5:1-20
MATTHEW 8:28-34; LUKE 8:26-40

Jesus and his disciples got into a boat and went to a place called the Gerasenes. It was a place where many Greek people lived and raised pigs. Jewish people thought the meat of pigs was not good, so they avoided pigs altogether.

When Jesus arrived on shore, a man with an evil spirit came out to him. This man lived in a nearby graveyard. He was mentally deranged and very dangerous. People were frightened of him and had tried to control him with chains, but he was so strong that he would pull the chains apart and break the irons that held his feet together. No one was strong enough to control him. Night and day he would cry out in agony as he ran around wildly, cutting himself on the rocks.

He will spare the poor and needy,

And will save the souls of the needy.

He will redeem their life from oppression and violence;

And precious shall be their blood in His sight.

PSALM 72:13-14

When the man saw Jesus, he ran to him, fell on his knees in front of Jesus, and screamed at the top of his voice, "Why did you come here, Jesus, Son of the Most High God? Swear that you won't torture me!"

Jesus knew the man had demons in him, so he called out to him, "Come out of this man, you evil spirit!"

Then Jesus asked the man, "What is your name?"

"I am called Legion!" he screamed, "because I have many, many demons in me." And he begged Jesus again and again to let him stay there and be left alone.

A large herd of pigs was eating grass and weeds on a nearby hillside. When the demons realized that Jesus was not going to leave them alone, they begged Jesus, "Send us into the pigs; we want to go into them." Jesus did so and the demons rushed out and entered the herd of pigs. All two thousand pigs in that herd immediately became uncontrollable and wild. They rushed down a steep hill and went into the lake and drowned themselves.

The men who had been watching over the pigs were in shock. They ran off and told this in the nearby villages. The people went out to see what the men were talking about. When they came to Jesus, they saw the man who had been demon-possessed sitting there in fresh clothes, looking calm and normal. The people were still afraid because their pigs were gone. Then those who had seen what had happened told the people that Jesus had driven the demons out of the man and sent them into the pigs. The people were very upset and begged Jesus to leave their town. They cared more about the pigs than about the man who had been rescued from the demons.

As Jesus started to get into the boat to leave, the man who had been demon-possessed begged to go with him. Jesus said, "No. I want you to go home to your family and tell them what the Lord did for you, and how he showed you mercy."

Although the man really wanted to follow Jesus, he knew he had to obey his new master. So the man went home to the Decapolis, an area of ten Greek towns, and told all his Greek friends and family how much Jesus, the Jewish Messiah, had done for him. The Greeks were amazed at what this Jewish prophet had done for this man who they knew had been possessed by demons.

By doing a miracle for someone who was not Jewish, Jesus showed that he had come to save all people, not just the Jews.

"I, the LORD, have called You in righteousness,

And will hold Your hand;

I will keep You and give You as a covenant to the people,

As a light to the Gentiles."

ISAIAH 42:6

THE BLEEDING WOMAN
& THE LITTLE GIRL WHO
WAS RAISED TO LIFE

MARK 5:22-43; MATTHEW 9:18-26
LUKE 8:40-56

After driving out demons from the man who lived in the graveyard, Jesus and his disciples sailed back across the Sea of Galilee to Capernaum. When they arrived, a large crowd was waiting for them on the shore. One of the men who was waiting, named Jairus, was the ruler of the synagogue. When Jesus landed, the man came and fell down before him and said, "My little daughter is dying. I love her so much. Please come and heal her body so that she will live."

So Jesus followed Jairus. As Jesus was going to his house, a large gathering of people pressed up very close to him. One of those in the crowd was a poor woman who had blood flowing out of her. She had suffered terribly for twelve years and she had seen many doctors. But they could not help her. Instead of getting better, she grew worse.

When she had heard that Jesus was in town, she came up behind him and stretched out her hand to touch his clothes. She was so desperate to be healed that she said to herself, "If I can just touch his clothes I know that he will make me well."

At that very moment her bleeding completely stopped. What she had been suffering from twelve years was taken away at last.

Now, many people were touching Jesus, but when he felt the woman's touch Jesus stopped immediately. He felt that some power had gone out from him. He turned around and asked, "Who touched me?"

The disciples were surprised by Jesus' question because everyone was touching him. "Teacher, how can you ask such a question? Everyone is trying to touch you!"

But Jesus knew that one person's touch was much different than all the others, and he kept looking for this person.

The woman realized what had happened, and she knew that Jesus was looking for her. She was afraid she might have done something wrong, and she came forward fearfully and fell before Jesus. Then she told him what had just happened. He smiled at her and said, "Dear daughter, your faith in me is what made you well. Get up now and go in peace and be free from this suffering."

While Jesus was talking with the woman, some men came up to Jairus and said to him, "I'm sorry to have to tell you this, but your daughter has died. There is no longer any need for you to bring Jesus to the house."

Jesus looked at Jarius's face. He was very sad because he really believed that if Jesus had arrived on time that he would heal his daughter. Jesus said, "Do not be afraid. You must continue to believe in me."

When they came to Jarius's home, all the people were crying loudly. But Jesus said to them, "There is no need to cry. The little girl is not dead, she is only asleep."

Did Jesus mean that although the child had really died, it was like sleep because Jesus was going to bring her back to life? Or did he mean that the child was not literally dead but only in a coma and that he would bring her out of it? Regardless of what he meant, the people started laughing at Jesus after he said this. They mocked him and showed that they did not believe Jesus could heal the child. So Jesus had them all leave the house at once.

Then he took the child's mother and father and Peter, James, and John and went into the room where child was lying. Taking the child's hand, he said to her, "Little girl, rise up!"

As soon as he said this, the child opened her eyes, got up from the bed, and walked around the room. The girl was just twelve years old.

Jesus told everyone in the room not to tell anyone what had happened. Then he told them, "Give the child something to eat."

So Little Food &
So Many People to Feed

MARK 6:7-12, 30-44
LUKE 9:1-17
MATTHEW 10:1-11:1, 14:14-21
JOHN 6:1-14

After Jesus healed Jairus's daughter, he sent his disciples on a mission throughout Galilee. Jesus told them to preach to the people that they should repent of their sins because the Kingdom of God was near. He also gave them power to heal the sick and drive out demons.

Jesus was now well known throughout the land, and now his disciples' preaching and doing miracles in his name made Jesus even more popular. The people were amazed at what the disciples could do. But they were not as amazed as the twelve disciples were themselves! They were astonished by the power that Jesus gave them and were more joyous than they had ever been in their lives. When they returned to Jesus, they reported all they had done and taught. One of them said, "Lord, even the demons submit to us."

Jesus said to them, "Yes, I gave you this power. But do not rejoice just because the demons submit to you. Rejoice because your names are written in heaven."

While they were giving their glowing reports about all that had happened, a huge crowd was growing around them.

So many people wanted their help that they did not even find a moment to get a bite to eat. Jesus then said to the twelve, "Let's get into the boat and go to a quiet place away from the crowd so that we can get some rest."

So they went away by boat to the other side of the lake. But the people saw them, and followed them along the shore, and figured out where they were going. They could see the boat in the distance and kept traveling as fast as they could along the lake until they arrived at the place where they knew Jesus would land. When Jesus came ashore he saw the huge crowds begging for his attention. Many of the people were sick and demon-possessed. When he saw this, his heart felt warm toward them like a parent whose small child is asking for help. He thought they were like sheep without a shepherd, so he began to help them and teach them many things about God.

As evening came near, his disciples said to Jesus: "This place is isolated. And the people are very hungry. What can we do to help them? Please, Jesus, send the people away so they can go to the nearby villages and buy themselves something to eat!"

But Jesus wanted to remind them of the power he had given them to help people. "Why do they need to go away? You can give them food to eat."

They did not understand what Jesus was talking about and were surprised to hear Jesus say this. "Are you serious? We would have to work eight months to earn enough money to buy enough bread for each of these people to have even a little."

Then Jesus realized how easily they had forgotten the power he had given them. So he asked them, "How many loaves of bread do you have?" When they hesitated he said, "Go quickly and see."

After the disciples went to see how much food they could find, they returned to Jesus and said, "Five loaves and two fish."

Then Jesus told the people to sit down on the grass in large groups. He took the five loaves and the two fish and looked up to give thanks to God. Then he broke the loaves and the fishes into pieces and gave them to his disciples. They put the pieces in baskets to distribute among all the thousands of people. But as they distributed what was in the baskets, more loaves and fishes would suddenly appear. The loaves and fishes continued to multiply until everyone had eaten all they wanted. Then the disciples picked up the leftovers. They gathered up so much that it filled up twelve basketfuls of broken pieces of bread and fish. Altogether they counted five thousand men who had eaten that day. And that did not take into account all the women and children who also ate.

Jesus Walks on the Water

Mark 6:45-52
Matthew 14:22-33
John 6:15-69

After Jesus had taken care of a large crowd's hunger with only five loaves and two fish, the great crowd of people was so impressed that they wanted Jesus to be their king. They hated the Romans and wanted to be free from Roman rule. They wanted Jesus to lead them in rebellion against Rome. Even his disciples wanted Jesus to lead the people in this way.

But Jesus wanted no part of this. He came to rule the hearts of men so they could live rightly before God. He had no intention to rule the people with soldiers and armies. So Jesus made his disciples get into a boat and go on ahead of him while he dismissed the crowd. After the crowd had dispersed, he went into the hills to be alone and to pray to his Father in heaven. He had planned to be there all night.

But while he was praying a fierce storm with howling winds came upon the lake. From his place on the hill he could see the disciples struggling mightily as they rowed their boat against a very strong wind.

At a little past midnight, when the storm was at its worst, Jesus walked down the mountain and to the shore. When he got to the water, he continued to walk. But he did not sink. He walked on top of the water! He continued to walk on the water toward the boat as the winds blew and the waves crashed. The disciples saw something coming toward them and they screamed in terror, for they thought they were seeing a ghost.

But Jesus called out. "Don't be afraid; it is I!"

When they heard his voice, Peter called out, "Lord, let me come to you on the water." Jesus said, "Come."

So Simon Peter climbed out of the boat and began to walk on the water just like Jesus. At first he was doing well, but then he took his eyes off Jesus and became afraid. At that moment he began to sink into the water. He screamed, "Lord, save me!"

Then Jesus reached out his hand, lifted Peter up out of the water, and brought Peter back to the boat. When they both climbed in, the storm died down and everything became calm and still. Jesus looked at Peter and the other disciples and said, "O you of little faith; why did you doubt me?'

The disciples were amazed at his words because even though Jesus had done so much with them, they still really didn't believe in his power. Their faith in Jesus was still small.

Soon after this Jesus came again to Capernaum and went into the synagogue.

Some of the people who had witnessed the miracle of the loaves and fishes were there. They asked him, "What does God require of us?"

Jesus answered, "God wants you to believe in the one he has sent."

The people were bothered by Jesus' words. They asked him, "What sign can you show that God has sent you? Moses gave our fathers bread from heaven in the desert. Show us what you can give."

Jesus said to them, "It was not Moses but God who gave your fathers bread in the desert. And God will give you true bread from heaven, through me, his Son who came down from heaven. He has come to give life."

Many of the people turned away and left him. Just a few days earlier they wanted to make him their king.

Jesus turned to his disciples and said, "What about you? Will you also walk away and leave me?'

Peter answered him, "Lord, where else can we go? You alone have the words of eternal life."

JESUS HEALS TWO GREEKS
& FEEDS FOUR THOUSAND MEN

MARK 7:24-8:10
MATTHEW 15:21-39

Jesus knew that very soon his disciples would be responsible for taking the gospel all over the world. Jesus needed time to prepare them for this task. So they traveled to a small village near Tyre and Sidon and away from the large crowds that followed him, so he could be alone with the twelve disciples to prepare them for what they must do. But wherever he went, he could not hide his presence.

A Greek woman came to Jesus greatly distraught because her beloved daughter had a demon in her. She cried out loudly for Jesus to drive out the demon.

The disciples said to Jesus, "Please, send this woman away. She is a distraction." The disciples thought that God was only going to save Jewish people. But Jesus had come to save everyone. This woman, even though she was not a Jew, was still loved by God. But Jesus had to fulfill God's plan of redemption in the order God had wanted—to the Jews first and then in time to all the other peoples on the face of the earth. So he said to this Greek woman, "I have been sent first to those who are lost in Israel."

But the woman kept pleading with Jesus to help her. Then Jesus said, "It is not right to take children's bread and give it to their dogs."

"Yes, Lord," she said, "but even the dogs eat the crumbs that fall from their masters' table." Jesus and his disciples were amazed at her words because she knew how powerful Jesus was and that it would take so little, even the equivalent of a crumb of his power, to cleanse her daughter from the evil spirit that had entered her.

Then Jesus looked at his disciples and then to the woman and said, "Go. The evil spirit has left your daughter."

The woman went home and found her daughter resting on the bed. And the evil spirit was gone from her body.

Jesus left that town and took his disciples to an area near where he had driven an army of demons out of a man and into a herd of pigs. At that time the people had told Jesus to leave their land. But now because of the great change in the man who had been healed—he went from being a horrible, frightening monster to a person who was kind and grateful for what Jesus had done—they all wanted to see Jesus.

When Jesus arrived they brought a man who was deaf and could not speak. They asked Jesus to help him. So Jesus took the man away from the crowd. Then he stuck his fingers into the man's ears and also touched his tongue. He looked up into the sky and said, "Be opened!"

At that moment the man's ears were opened, his tongue became loose, and he began to speak plainly. Jesus told the people not to tell anyone, but they were so amazed at what Jesus had done that they told everyone they could. They said of Jesus, "He does all things so well. He even gives hearing to the deaf and helps mute people to speak!"

So despite Jesus' efforts to be alone with his disciples, a great many people followed him to hear him teach and to be healed of sickness and demon possession. After a few days the little food that they had was all gone. Jesus called his disciples to him and said, "I'm concerned for these people; they have been with me three days and now have nothing to eat. We can't send them home hungry because some of them will not have enough strength to go on such a journey from here back to their homes. They will collapse on the way."

His disciples seemed to have short memories. They answered, "But where in this place so far away from the towns will we find enough bread to feed all these people?"

Jesus was amazed at how little they remembered from the time that he had fed five thousand with just five loaves and two fish. "How many loaves do you have?" Jesus asked.

Then they remembered and said, "Seven!"

Jesus took the seven loaves and a few small fish, gave thanks, broke the bread, and gave it to his disciples to set before the people. He gave thanks for them and told the disciples to distribute them. Just like when he satisfied the five thousand with five loaves and two fish, this time he satisfied four thousand men. The disciples picked up seven baskets of leftover bread and fish.

Then Jesus sent the crowds home so that he could be alone with his disciples, for he had so many things he wanted to teach them.

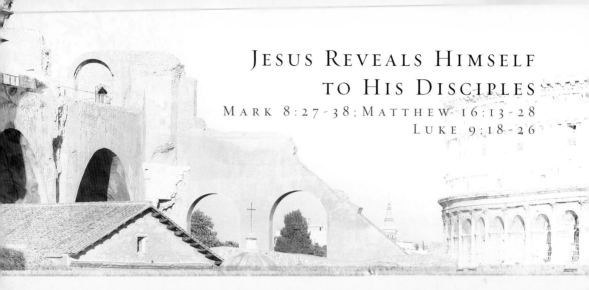

JESUS REVEALS HIMSELF TO HIS DISCIPLES

MARK 8:27-38; MATTHEW 16:13-28
LUKE 9:18-26

After Jesus had again fed a large crowd with just a few pieces of bread and fish, he and his disciples went to a place called Caesarea Philippi. When he was alone with his disciples he asked them, "Who do men say that I am?"

They answered him, "Some say that you are John the Baptist. Others say you are the prophet Elijah."

Then Jesus asked, "What about you? Who do you say I am?"

Simon Peter stared directly at Jesus. Then he fell on his knees in front of him and said, "You are the Christ, the Messiah who we have been waiting for, the Son of the living God!"

Jesus said to Peter, "This knowledge has not come to you on your own. My Father in heaven has revealed this to you." Then Jesus said, "Peter, your confession is the rock of faith on which I will build my church. All the power of evil in the world will not overcome it."

Jesus said this because he would build his church on the faith of people who really believed and would publicly confess, like Peter, that Jesus is the Christ, the Savior of the world.

Then Jesus began to tell his disciples some troubling things that would soon take place. "We are going up to Jerusalem, and the Son of Man" (that is what Jesus liked to call himself) "will be falsely accused as a liar, arrested, and beaten by the religious leaders and chiefs priests. They will have him killed. But after three days of being dead and buried he will be raised to life again."

The disciples were shocked by Jesus' teaching. They could not believe that such things would happen to Jesus. They still had in mind that Jesus would be made king and rule over all of Israel. They thought that they would be given high places of authority in this new kingdom and rule along with Jesus.

Peter was so upset that he took Jesus aside and said to him firmly, "Teacher, you mustn't say things like that. You will not suffer and die. You will be king!"

But Jesus knew that Peter was speaking thoughts that Satan, the evil one, had placed in his heart. Satan knew the plan that God had sent Jesus to fulfill, and he was using Peter to try to persuade Jesus not to go forward with this plan.

Then Jesus became angry and said to Peter, "Get away from me, Satan! You are trying to be a stumbling block to keep me from carrying out God's will. Your words do not come from the mind of God but from the mind of men!"

God did not send Jesus to be an earthly ruler or king. God sent Jesus to die on the cross to save the world from sin. Jesus wanted to make this plain to all his disciples and followers. So he called all of them together and said: "If anyone wants to be my disciple, he must follow my example and be willing to take up the cross that God has given him. For whoever is willing to give up his life for my sake will be saved. But if he is not willing to give his life for me or the gospel, he will lose his life. What good is it if a man gains everything in the whole world but loses his own soul?

"If anyone is ashamed of me and my words in this sinful world, I will be ashamed of him when I return again from heaven in God's glory with the holy angels."

THE GLORY OF JESUS
ON THE MOUNTAIN

MARK 9:2-32
MATTHEW 17:1-23
LUKE 9:28-45; 2 PETER 1:16-18

About a week after Jesus told his disciples how he was going to die, he called Peter, James, and John to climb a high mountain with him. When they came to a special place on the mountain, Jesus' body began to change from its normal color to a body that began to glow like a brilliant white light. His face and clothes became so dazzling in their whiteness that it was hard to look at him.

Then two men appeared with Jesus on the mountain. They were the great prophets Moses and Elijah who had come down from heaven to talk with Jesus.

Peter was amazed that these men who he had heard about in Bible stories were now right in front of him! He was both afraid and confused and said, "Teacher, thank you for allowing us to see this! Let us build three altars so that we can worship you, Moses, and Elijah!" He had no idea what he was saying because the heavenly glory that glowed from Jesus, Moses, and Elijah was beyond his ability to understand.

And if that wasn't enough, a huge cloud came over them and a powerful voice, the voice of God, came from the cloud and said, "This is my beloved Son. Listen carefully to him!"

When the disciples heard this they fell to the ground in fear, even more terrified than before. When they finally looked up they saw that the cloud was gone and no one was there except Jesus.

As they walked down the mountain together, Jesus told them not to tell anyone what they had just experienced until after he was raised from the dead. They didn't say a word to anyone about what they had seen. And they had no idea what "raised from the dead" meant.

When they came down the mountain, they found the other nine disciples engaged in a heated argument with one man. Many people were around them, listening. When Jesus arrived the people ran toward him and were amazed to see him. It was as if some of the glow from the mountain lingered.

Then the man who had been arguing with the disciples said to Jesus: "Teacher, I brought my son to your disciples because an evil spirit has taken him. He is a good boy and I love him. Since the spirit has entered him he can no longer speak. It slams him to the ground. He shakes violently, growls, and foams out spit and saliva from his mouth. I asked your disciples to drive the evil spirit out, but they could not do it!"

Then Jesus said to everyone, "How long shall I put up with your unbelief? Bring the boy here to me."

As soon as the evil spirit saw Jesus, it slammed the boy to the ground, and it looked like the spirit was tearing the boy apart.

Jesus asked the boy's father, "How long has this evil spirit been in him?"

"Ever since he was a little child," the boy's father said. "But if you have the power to do anything, please have mercy on us and do something!"

"If I have the power?" said Jesus. "All things are possible to those who believe in me!"

At that moment the father gave out a desperate cry for help. "I DO BELIEVE!" Then he looked at the boy and in great distress turned to Jesus and said, "But how can I believe when I see my boy like this? HELP ME OVERCOME MY UNBELIEF!"

The crowd heard the father's scream and came running to see what all the yelling was about. When Jesus saw the crowd he turned to the evil spirit and commanded it, "Come out of this boy and never go into him again!"

At that moment the spirit screamed and with enormous force slammed the boy to the ground one last time and then came out. The boy just lay there motionless for several moments. He looked like he might be dead.

But Jesus knelt down and helped him to his feet. The boy stood up. Everyone saw that he was completely healed. Jesus gave him to his father who was overwhelmed with joy.

Then Jesus decided to leave that place so that he could be alone with his disciples and tell them more about God's plan to save all people. Jesus taught them, "One of you will betray me into the hands of those who want to destroy me. They will kill me. But after three days I will rise again. This is God's plan that I must carry out."

The disciples had no idea what he was talking about. But they did not feel comfortable asking him questions about it.

LAZARUS RAISED TO LIFE

JOHN 11:1-55

While Jesus was preaching to the people beyond the Jordan, his close friends Mary and Martha sent word to him that their brother, Lazarus, was very ill. Jesus loved Lazarus, but he stayed where he was another two days before he said to his disciples, "We must go back to Judea, near Jerusalem."

The disciples were surprised to hear this because Jesus had been avoiding Judea and Jerusalem where the Jews had been seeking to kill him.

Jesus said, "Our friend Lazarus has fallen asleep, but I must go to awake him."

The disciples said, "Master, if he is asleep, surely he will awaken soon."

"Lazarus is dead," Jesus said. "But let us go to him so that you will see my power and believe in me even more."

When they arrived at Bethany, about two miles from Jerusalem, they learned that Lazarus had been dead for four days. Martha came out to meet Jesus. She was deeply distressed and said, "Lord, if you had come earlier, my brother would not have died."

Jesus said to her, "Your brother shall rise again."

"I know that he will rise again at the resurrection," Martha said.

Then Jesus said, "Whoever believes in me will never die. Do you believe this?"

She said to him, "Yes, Lord, I believe that you are the Christ, the Son of God, who has come into the world."

Then Martha went into the house to get her sister Mary. "The Teacher is here!"

At once Mary rose up to go to Jesus. She fell down at his feet and said, "Lord, if you had been here, my brother would not have died!"

When Jesus saw Mary weeping, his heart was filled with sorrow. He saw how the death of a loved one causes so much pain. He felt deep sorrow in his heart. But he also became angry at the pain and anguish that sin and death cause. He realized even more deeply that eradicating death was one reason that God had sent him into the world.

Jesus asked, "Where have you laid him?"

They showed him the cave where Lazarus was buried. It had a stone over the opening. All the people saw Jesus stand near the cave and weep because of his love for Lazarus. But a few people mocked Jesus and said, "If this man can make the blind see, then why didn't he keep this man from dying?"

Then Jesus said in a loud, angry voice, "Move away the stone!"

Martha said, "Lord, his body has been in there for four days. When you move the stone the smell will be horrible."

As they took away the stone Jesus prayed to his Father in heaven, "Father, I do this so the people standing here may believe that you sent me."

Then Jesus called out in a loud voice, "Lazarus, come out!"

As soon as he said this, the man who had been dead for four days came out of the tomb. The people were amazed and shocked. His body still had strips of burial cloth on him.

Jesus said, "Take off his grave clothes and let him go."

When the people saw this, they believed. News of this traveled fast and reached the ears of the Jewish leaders in Jerusalem. They called a meeting of all the rulers of the Jews.

"What shall we do?" they asked. "This man is performing many miracles. Soon they will try to make him king of Israel. Then they will rebel against Rome, and the Romans will destroy our nation."

Then the high priest Caiaphas said, "It is better that one man die for the people than for our whole nation be destroyed. This man must die." The high priest did not realize that this was the plan all along. He said this because he had evil intent. But God had planned this to save the world.

From that day on all the rulers agreed to find a way to have Jesus killed.

JUDAS MAKES A DEAL WITH THE CHIEF PRIESTS

MARK 14:1-11
MATTHEW 26:6-16
LUKE 22:1-6; JOHN 12:1-11

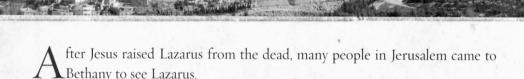

After Jesus raised Lazarus from the dead, many people in Jerusalem came to Bethany to see Lazarus.

But the rulers of the Jews said, "We must not only kill Jesus but Lazarus also because so many of the people believe in Jesus because of him."

Bethany was only two miles from Jerusalem. Jesus' friends who lived there had a dinner in his honor at the home of Simon the Leper. Jesus came with his disciples, and Lazarus, Mary, and Martha were also there.

While they were at the supper, Mary the sister of Lazarus came into the room with a jar of very expensive perfume. She opened the jar and poured the perfume on Jesus' head and feet. Then she wiped his feet with her long hair.

Judas Iscariot, one of the disciples, was angered by this. "This is such a waste of money! The perfume could have been sold for more than a year's salary and the money given to the poor!"

Judas really didn't care for the poor. He was the one who kept the money for Jesus and the twelve. He often took some of the money for his own use and didn't tell anyone.

But Jesus said: "Leave her alone. Why are you troubling this woman? She has done a beautiful thing for me. The poor you will always have with you, and you can give to them anytime you want. But you will not always have me. She did what she could. She poured perfume on my body beforehand to prepare for my burial. Listen to me, everyone. Wherever the gospel is preached throughout the world, what this woman has done will also be told in memory of her."

Mary knew that Jesus would soon be killed. So she honored him by showing her love and affection with this gift and act of humble worship.

But Judas was very angry at this. At his first opportunity he went to the chief priests to find out what they would pay if he helped to have Jesus arrested.

They said, "We will give you thirty pieces of silver."

Judas agreed on the price and began looking for an opportunity to help the religious authorities arrest Jesus.

Palm Sunday

MARK 11:1-11
MATTHEW 21:1-11
LUKE 19:28-40; JOHN 12:12-19

Just before Jesus entered Jerusalem he called two of his disciples and said to them, "Go into the next village and you will find a colt tied there. Untie it and bring it to me. If anyone asks, 'Why are you doing this?' Tell him, 'the Lord needs it, and he will return it soon.'"

They went to the place, found the colt, and began to untie it. Some people there thought they were stealing it. They said, "What are you doing? That colt isn't yours!" But the disciples answered just as Jesus told them to, and the people were satisfied.

They brought the colt to Jesus and placed their clothes on the back of it as a saddle. Jesus sat on it and began to ride into Jerusalem. A great crowd greeted him because Jesus was by now very well known. They showed respect for him by spreading some of their clothes on the ground to make a path for him. Others waved branches from palm trees.

They all shouted in loud voices:

"Hosanna! Blessed is he who comes in the name of the Lord!"

"Blessed is the coming kingdom of our father David!"

"Hosanna in the highest!"

They said this because they believed that Jesus had come as a conquering king of Israel, like David of old, and would save them from Roman tyranny.

Some of the Pharisees were furious with the crowd and said to Jesus, "Teacher, tell your disciples to be quiet."

Jesus answered them by saying, "I tell you the truth, if they should be quiet, the very stones on the ground would cry out!"

When he came into Jerusalem with this multitude, he went into the temple and looked around. He knew that this was his Father's house. And he knew that God had sent him to Jerusalem for a very special purpose. Now was the time for that purpose to be completed. All this took place on the Sunday five days before Jesus' death. It is called Palm Sunday because it marks how Jesus was greeted with palm branches by all the people as Jesus entered Jerusalem just a few days before he was crucified.

"Rejoice greatly, O daughter of Zion!
Shout, O daughter of Jerusalem!
Behold, your King is coming to you;
He is just and having salvation,
Lowly and riding on a donkey,
A colt, the foal of a donkey.

ZECHARIAH 9:9

JESUS CHALLENGES THE
LEADERS IN JERUSALEM

MARK 11:15-20, 11:27-33, 12:1-17
MATTHEW 21:12-17, 21:23-27, 21:33-46
·LUKE 19:45-20:26

The day after Palm Sunday, Jesus returned to Jerusalem. He went back into the temple that Monday morning and saw many people buying and selling there. It looked more like an open market than a place of worship. He became angry and began to turn over the tables of those collecting money and drove away those who were selling doves to be offered as a sacrifice for sins. Then he said, "My house shall be called a house of prayer for all nations, but you have made it a den of thieves!"

The chief priests and the teachers of the law saw this and became furious. They began plotting among themselves how they might kill Jesus. But because they saw how many people were coming to hear Jesus teach, they knew that there was nothing they could do at that time.

Jesus taught all day long. In the evening he went back to Bethany with his disciples.

The next morning, the Tuesday before Passover, Jesus again came to the temple courts in Jerusalem. The chief priests, the teachers of the law, and the elders came to him.

They said, "Who gave you authority to come in here and disrupt our temple?"

Jesus replied, "I will ask you one question. Answer me, and I will tell you the authority that I have. The baptism for repentance that John preached in the desert—did it come from God, or did John just make it up?

They discussed it among themselves and said, "If we say, 'From God,' he will ask, 'why didn't you believe John?' But if we say, 'It came from him' the people will be angry because they respected John as a prophet sent from God."

So they answered Jesus, "We don't know."

Jesus said, "Then I will not tell you by what authority I am doing these things."

He then began to tell them a story that would answer the question about where his authority came from.

"A man planted a vineyard. He put a wall around it and built a watchtower to protect it. Then he rented the vineyard to some farmers and went away on a journey. After a long time he sent one of his servants to collect from the farmers some of the fruit of the vineyard. But instead of welcoming him and treating him with respect, they beat him and sent him back to the owner of the vineyard with nothing.

Then the owner sent another servant to them, and they did the same thing. He sent a third servant. That one they killed. Over time he sent many other servants, but the farmers either beat or killed them all.

"Finally the owner had only one person left to send. It was his son whom he loved. He sent him last of all saying, 'They will respect my son.'

"But the farmers said to one another, 'This is the son. Let's kill him, and then when the owner dies there will be no heir. The inheritance will be ours.' So they took the son, and killed him, and threw him out of the vineyard.

"What then will the owner do? He will come himself and kill those farmers and give the vineyard to others. Haven't you read this scripture? 'The stone the builders rejected has become the capstone; the Lord has done this, and it is wonderful in our eyes.'"

Then the religious leaders looked for a way to arrest him because they knew he had spoken the story against them. But they were afraid of the crowd, so they left him and went away.

Later they sent some of the religious leaders to Jesus to try to trick him. They came to him and said: "Teacher, we know you are a man of integrity. You don't change your beliefs because of popular opinion; you teach the way of God in accordance with the truth. So let us ask you this question. Is it right for us Jews to pay taxes to Caesar? Should we pay or shouldn't we?"

But Jesus could see through this trap. If he said "pay taxes to Caesar," these men would say Jesus was a friend of the Romans and an enemy to the Jewish people.

The people would no longer follow and would despise him. But if he said "do not pay taxes to Caesar," they would tell the Roman government that Jesus was causing a rebellion, and they would instantly arrest Jesus for treason. Either way his answer could be used against him. So he said, "Why are you trying to trap me? Bring me a Roman coin and let me look at it." When they brought a coin he asked them, "Whose portrait is on the coin?

"Caesar's," they replied.

Then Jesus said to them, "Then give to Caesar what belongs to Caesar. And give to God what belongs to God."

And they were amazed at him because he gave an answer that could not be used against him.

The Spirit of the LORD shall rest upon Him,

The Spirit of wisdom and understanding,

The Spirit of counsel and might,

The Spirit of knowledge and of the fear of the LORD.

ISAIAH 11:2

THE GREATEST COMMANDMENT

MARK 12:28-12:44, MATTHEW 22:34-45; LUKE 20:41-21:4

While Jesus was debating the religious leaders about his authority to teach the people, one of the teachers of the law noticed how well Jesus had answered all of their questions. So he asked, "Of all the commandments God has given us, which is the most important?"

Jesus looked at him to see if the man was asking this question honestly or if he was only trying to trick him like the others. Then he said, "The most important one is this: 'Hear, O Israel, the LORD our God, the LORD is one. Love the LORD your God with all your heart and with all your soul and with all your mind and with all your strength.' The second is this: 'Love your neighbor as yourself.' There are no greater commands than these."

"Hear, O Israel: The LORD our God, the LORD is one! You shall love the LORD your God with all your heart, with all your soul, and with all your strength."

DEUTERONOMY 6 : 4 - 5

After Jesus said this, the man looked at Jesus closely and replied, "Well answered, teacher. It is true that there is only one God and no other. To love him with all your heart, with all your understanding, and with all your strength, and to love your neighbor as yourself is more important than all our religious practices and offerings."

When Jesus saw that the man had answered well, he said to him, "You are not far from the kingdom of God." And from then on no one dared to ask Jesus any more questions.

When he saw that no one was challenging him, Jesus spoke again about his authority to teach. He asked this question: "How is it that the religious leaders say that the one who God has promised to send will be a son of David?" (People expected the Messiah to be one of David's descendants.) "David himself wrote in his prayer book, the Psalms, 'God said to the one I call my Lord: "Sit at my right side next to me until I put all your enemies under your rule." If David calls the one God will send 'my Lord,' how can he be his son?"

Jesus said this to make sure that the people understood that he was greater than David, the man who the people looked up to most. The person David looked up to and worshiped was Jesus.

Jesus also taught the people this: "Watch out for the religious leaders. They like to be looked up to and treated with honor in public places. They rob widows of their inheritance, and they say lengthy prayers just to show how religious they are. God will judge these men harshly."

Then Jesus sat down near the place where people put their money into the temple treasury. He saw many rich people put in large amounts. But he also saw a poor widow put in two small coins worth less than a penny.

Jesus was impressed by this and called his disciples to him and said, "This poor woman has put more into the treasury than all the others combined. They all gave from their wealth; but she sacrificed out of her poverty, everything—all she had to live on."

". . . you shall love your neighbor as yourself: I am the LORD."

LEVITICUS 19:18

Jesus Predicts the Last Days on Earth

Mark 13:1-37 Matthew 24:1-25:46; Luke 21:5-36

As Jesus left the temple that day, one of his disciples was greatly impressed by the size and beauty of all the buildings and said, "Look, Teacher! What massive stones! What magnificent buildings!"

Jesus replied, "Not one stone of this temple will be left on another; every one will be destroyed."

When they came to the Mount of Olives that overlooked the city and the temple, Peter, James, John, and Andrew asked Jesus, "When will the temple be destroyed?"

Jesus said to them: "In the days to come be careful that you are not misled. Listen carefully to my teaching. As I have said, know for certain that I will die and rise again.

"In God's time I will come again with great power. But when I am gone many will try to deceive you. They will use my name and say 'I am he.' But that will not be true.

"In the days to come there will be many wars between nations. People will see earthquakes and famines. Such things will happen, but that does not mean the end is at hand.

"You must be very alert. In the days to come you will be handed over to the government authorities and punished because you are my disciples. You will be taken before governors and kings to tell them about me, because it is God's plan that the gospel must first be preached to all nations on earth before I come again. As you tell the world about me, many will resist you and arrest you and bring you to trial. Do not worry about what to say; just listen to the Holy Spirit I will leave within you. He will give you the right words to say.

"Those days will be dreadful. Brothers will betray their brothers, and fathers will betray their children because of me. Those days will be worse than any days since God created the world. If the Lord did not see fit to shorten those days, no one could survive. But for the sake of the ones he has chosen, he has shortened them.

"At that time if anyone says 'here is the Christ!' or 'there he is!' do not believe it. False Christs will appear and perform signs and miracles to try to deceive those whom God has chosen. But that will not be possible. But be prepared; I am giving you this warning.

"After those terrible days people will see the Son of Man coming in clouds with great power and glory. And he will send his angels and gather his chosen from the ends of the earth to the ends of the heavens.

"No one knows when that day will come. The angels do not know, nor do I, but only the Father. So be ready! You do not know when it will happen. It's like a man leaving his home to go on a journey. He gives his servants work to do, and he tells them to have everything in order when he returns. His return could be at any time and without warning. When he arrives he must not find anyone asleep or unprepared. What I say to you now, I say to everyone who reads this:

"'Be prepared for my return!'"

"I am the Alpha and the Omega, the Beginning and the End," says the Lord,
"who is and who was and who is to come, the Almighty."

REVELATION 1:8

"And behold, I am coming quickly, and My reward is with Me, to give to every one according to his work. I am the Alpha and the Omega, the Beginning and the End, the First and the Last."

REVELATION 22:12-13

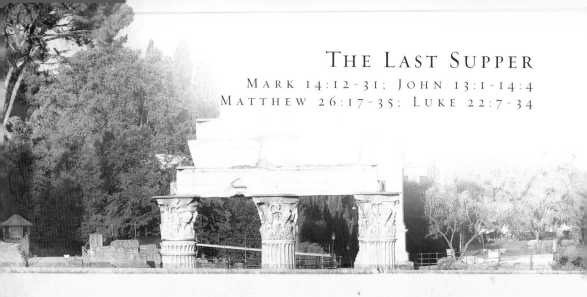

THE LAST SUPPER

MARK 14:12-31; JOHN 13:1-14:4
MATTHEW 26:17-35; LUKE 22:7-34

On the day before Jesus was arrested, he sent Peter and John to prepare a final meal for him to eat with his disciples. "Go into Jerusalem," he said, "and a man carrying a pitcher of water will meet you. Follow him, and go to the house where he leads you, and say to the owner, 'The teacher asks, "where is the guest room where I may eat the Passover meal with my disciples?"' He will show you an upper room ready for you to make the preparations."

They followed his instructions and found things just as Jesus had told them. When they arrived they prepared the Passover meal of vegetables, bread baked without yeast, and a roasted lamb.

In the evening, Jesus arrived with the twelve. The meal was already placed on a table with couches where each could lay down with his head near the table. Their bare feet lay exposed at the other end of the couch.

While they were reclining at the table, Jesus took bread, prayed to his Father in heaven, and broke it. He gave it to each of the disciples, saying, "Take it; this is my body." Then he poured wine into a cup, again gave thanks, and offered it to each of them, and they all drank from the same cup. "By my blood we will establish a new relationship between God and his people."

Then Jesus rose up and tied a long towel around his waist. He poured water into a bowl, carried it to each disciple, and one by one began to wash their feet.

When he came to Simon Peter, Peter said to him, "Lord, you are not going to wash my feet. I will never let you wash my feet."

"If you do not let me wash your feet," said Jesus, "then you are not one of my disciples."

After hearing this, Peter changed his tone. "Lord, if that is the case, don't wash just my feet, but my hands and my head as well!"

But Jesus replied, "No, Peter. You are clean. You only need to wash your feet to stay clean. But not all of you are clean."

Jesus was referring to Judas. He knew that Judas had made arrangements with the chief priests and would soon betray him to his enemies.

When he had finished washing the disciples' feet, he put away the towel and said, "You call me 'Master' and 'Lord,' and so I am. If as your Lord and Master, I have washed your feet, you should stay humble and be prepared to wash each other's feet."

Then Jesus looked at the disciples and said, "I know that one of you will betray me—one who is here eating with me."

They were saddened, and one by one said to him, "Surely not I?"

"It is one of the twelve," he said, "one who dips bread into the bowl with me." Then Jesus said to Judas, "Do quickly what you are going to do."

Judas went out at once. He knew that after supper Jesus would head back to Bethany by following a path near the Mount of Olives, so he went to the chief priests and led a band of men to betray Jesus there.

When Judas left, Jesus turned to the eleven disciples and said, "I will be with you only for a little while longer. Where I go, you cannot yet come."

The disciples were very sad to hear this so Jesus said, "You do not need to be troubled. Trust God. But trust also in me. In my Father's house are many rooms. I am going there to prepare a place for you. And when it is ready, I will come back to take you to be with me."

Jesus talked with his disciples and taught them many things. They prayed and sang together until midnight. Then they went out to the Mount of Olives.

"You will all fall away," Jesus told them, "but after I have risen from the dead, I will meet you in Galilee."

Peter declared, "Even if everyone falls away, I will not."

"I tell you the truth," Jesus answered, "today—yes, tonight—before the rooster crows twice you will disown me three times."

But Peter insisted, "Even if I have to die with you, I would never disown you." And all the others said the same.

In all their affliction He was afflicted,

And the Angel of His Presence saved them;

In His love and in His pity He redeemed them;

And He bore them and carried them

All the days of old.

ISAIAH 63:9

THE NIGHT JESUS WAS ARRESTED

MARK 14:32-54, 66-72; JOHN 18:1-27
MATTHEW 26:36-56, 69-75
LUKE 22:39-62

At the foot of the Mount of Olives, near the path toward Bethany, there was a shady grove of olive trees called the Garden of Gethsemane. Jesus and his disciples had been there before. When they arrived this late evening, Jesus called Simon Peter, James, and John to go with him a little farther into the garden.

Jesus knew that Judas and his armed men would arrive soon to arrest him. He also knew that he would be beaten and taken away to a brutal death. He said to his disciples, "My soul is filled with deep dread and sorrow. Keep watch while I pray."

He went a little farther and flung himself down to the ground and cried out:

"Father, if possible, let this pass from me. But do, not as I want, but as you want!"

His suffering was so great that drops of blood dripped from his face. When he finished praying he went back to the three disciples and found them not alert but asleep.

He shook Peter and said, "Simon, could you not stay awake with me for one hour? The spirit is willing, but the body is weak."

He went out a second time and prayed again. When he returned his disciples were still sleeping. But this time he did not wake them. He went out once more. When he returned the third time he seemed stronger and ready to face the awful things that were about to happen to him.

He looked at the three disciples and said gently, "Are you still sleeping and resting?"

Then he noticed movement along the path with people coming toward him. Jesus said, "The hour has come. I am now betrayed into the hands of sinners."

As soon as he said this, Judas arrived with his band of men. They were carrying swords and clubs. Judas came forward and kissed Jesus as a sign to the armed men that the one he kissed was the one they should arrest.

After the kiss, the men seized Jesus and arrested him. Peter drew his sword and struck one of the men and cut off his right ear.

Jesus said to Peter, "Put your the sword away."

Then he said to those who came with Judas, "Am I leading a rebellion? Do you need swords and clubs to arrest me? Every day I was teaching in the temple and you did not arrest me. But the Scriptures must be fulfilled."

He is despised and rejected by men,

A Man of sorrows and acquainted with grief.

And we hid, as it were, our faces from Him;

He was despised, and we did not esteem Him.

ISAIAH 53:3

Then all the disciples scattered and left Jesus all alone.

The soldiers took Jesus to the high priest, and all the religious leaders met together to determine what they could do to him.

Peter followed Jesus to the home of the high priest. In the courtyard the guards made a fire. He stood there with them by the fire to stay warm.

One of the servant girls of the house saw Peter by the fire and recognized him. She said, "You are one of the followers of that man Jesus from Nazareth."

Peter was surprised. He answered firmly, "Woman, I do not know what you are talking about." And he walked away.

And the woman said to those standing nearby, "This man is one of Jesus' disciples!" But Peter denied it again.

Later some of the men by the fire noticed that Peter's accent was like those who live in the region around Sea of Galilee. They said, "You must be one of them. Your speech gives you away. You are a Galilean just as they are."

Peter cursed at them and yelled out, "I don't know this man!" As soon as he said this, he heard a rooster crow for the second time.

Then Peter remembered the words Jesus had spoken to him only a few short hours earlier: "Before the rooster crows twice, you will deny me three times."

Then Peter broke down and wept.

JESUS IS CONDEMNED TO DIE

MARK 14:55-65,
15:1-20
MATTHEW 27:1-31
LUKE 22:63-23:25
JOHN 18:28-19:16

Jesus' enemies tried to make a case against Jesus. They had men testify that Jesus had made blasphemous statements that would give them grounds to have him executed. But they found nothing. Some men swore one thing and some swore another, but their words did not agree.

Jesus stood there bound with cords around his hands as the people accused him of many false charges. Finally the high priest stood up and said to Jesus, "Have you nothing to say. How do you defend yourself against these charges?"

But Jesus did not say anything in his defense.

Then the high priest asked him, "Are you the Christ, the Son of God?"

Jesus said, "I am. And you will see the Son of Man sitting on the right hand of

God and coming in the clouds of heaven!"

When the high priest heard this, he was furious. He looked around and exclaimed: "We don't need any witnesses! Did you hear what he said? He claims to be God's Son? What should we do!"

With one voice they all said, "Put him to death!"

Some started to spit on him. Others blindfolded him, struck him with their fists, and mocked him by demanding that Jesus tell them who had hit him even though he was blindfolded and could not see. Then the guards led him out of the room and beat him again.

Meanwhile, Judas Iscariot was horrified. He did not believe that they would put Jesus to death. But when he saw Jesus bound and beaten, Judas realized that he had done a terrible deed by betraying Jesus. So he brought back the thirty pieces of silver that the rulers had given him to betray Jesus and said, "I have sinned in betraying an innocent man!"

But they answered him, "What is that to us?"

Judas took the thirty pieces of silver they gave him to betray Jesus and threw it in the temple. Then he went out and hanged himself.

The rulers took the money and bought a field to bury strangers who had no friends or family in the city.

The Lord GOD has opened My ear;

And I was not rebellious,

Nor did I turn away.

I gave My back to those who struck Me,

And My cheeks to those who plucked out the beard;

I did not hide My face from shame and spitting.

ISAIAH 50:5-6

Even though the rulers condemned Jesus, they could not put anyone to death unless they first received permission from the Roman governor. The governor at the time was a man named Pontius Pilate.

So, early in the morning the rulers and a crowd of people brought Jesus bound with cords to Pilate. Pilate asked them, "What charge do you bring against this man?"

The Jews said: "We have found this man teaching blasphemies and stirring up trouble in Jerusalem. He calls himself the Son of God and says he is a king. He tells our people not to pay taxes to Caesar. Your law does not allow us to put anyone to death, so we have brought him to you."

Then Pilate went to Jesus and said, "Are you the King of the Jews?"

Jesus answered, "My kingdom is not of this world."

Pilate said, "Are you a king then?"

Jesus answered him, "You are right in saying I am a king. For this reason was I born. For this I have come into the world."

Then, without waiting for an answer, Pilate went out to the rulers and said, "I find no reason to put this man to death."

But they cried out all the more, saying, "He stirs up the people everywhere to rebellion."

Now it was the custom that Pilate release a prisoner during the feast of the Passover. And at that time there was in the prison a man named Barabbas who had committed murder in an earlier rebellion against the Romans.

Pilate said to the people, "Shall I set Jesus free, the one you call the King of the Jews?"

But the rulers urged the crowd to ask Pilate to release Barabbas instead of Jesus.

So Pilate asked, "What shall I do with Jesus?"

And they all cried out, "Crucify him!"

Pilate could not believe it. But because he was weak he let the crowd pressure him to condemn an innocent man to be crucified on the cross. Then Pilate, to please the crowd, released Barabbas and handed Jesus over to be flogged.

The soldiers led Jesus away. They put a purple robe on Jesus and made a crown of thorns and set it on him. Then they mocked him by calling out, "Hail, king of the Jews!" They beat him repeatedly on the head with a staff and spit on him. Then they took off the purple robe, put his own clothes on him, and led him out to crucify him.

Surely He has borne our griefs

And carried our sorrows;

Yet we esteemed Him stricken,

Smitten by God, and afflicted.

But He was wounded for our transgressions,

He was bruised for our iniquities;

The chastisement for our peace was upon Him,

And by His stripes we are healed.

ISAIAH 53:4-5

THE DAY CHRIST DIED

MARK 15:20-39
MATTHEW 27:32-56
LUKE 23:26-49
JOHN 19:17-30

The Roman soldiers took Jesus out of the city to a hill called Golgotha, the place where they crucified criminals. A large crowd followed. The weight of the cross was too heavy for Jesus to bear because he was so weak from being beaten. So the soldiers grabbed a man who was visiting Jerusalem and made him carry Jesus' cross up the hill to the place of death.

When they arrived they laid the cross down on the ground and stretched Jesus' body over it. Then they drove nails through his hands and feet into the cross. After they did this, they stood the cross upright. Jesus was still conscious and could see the people below looking up at him.

It was about nine o'clock in the morning when they crucified him. A sign was posted on the cross that declared the charge against Jesus. It read: THE KING OF THE

JEWS. The chief priests did not like the sign and wanted Pilate to change it to "He claimed to be the King of the Jews." But Pilate would not change it.

The soldiers offered Jesus some wine mixed with myrrh, a kind of medicine to help deaden the pain. But he would not take it. He wanted his mind clear even though it meant that he would feel greater suffering.

The crowd looked up at him and mocked him, saying, "So! You are going to destroy the temple and rebuild it in three days. Then come down from the cross and save yourself!" Even the religious leaders mocked him: "He saved others. But he cannot save himself! Let this supposed Christ, this King of the Jews, come down now from the cross so we will see and believe."

Even as they mocked him Jesus prayed, "Father, forgive them; for they know not what they do."

They crucified two robbers with him, one on each side of him with Jesus in the middle. One of the robbers also mocked him. "If you are the Christ, save yourself and save us!"

But the other robber said, "Have you no fear of God! We deserve to die, but this man has done nothing wrong."

Then he said to Jesus, "Lord, remember me when you come into your kingdom!"

While they hung on their crosses about to die, Jesus promised him, "Today you shall be with me in paradise."

At noon darkness filled the whole sky for the next three hours. At three o'clock in the afternoon it was dark like midnight. Jesus had endured six hours of horrendous pain. At that moment he cried out, "My God, my God, why have you forsaken me!"

When he said these words, the great plan that God had sent Jesus to do was finally being accomplished. Jesus was absorbing the sins of the world onto himself. That was the reason Jesus came to earth. God saw innocent Jesus being changed by sin into the ugliest, most gruesome creature the universe had ever seen. It made God turn away for a moment. The agony that Jesus was experiencing was more than he could bear. The circle of love that the Father and the Son enjoyed from the beginning of time was now broken for the first and only time. They planned this separation to make it possible for people like you and me to join the circle of love with them. But in order for that to happen the sins of the world had to be paid for. God showed his love for us this way. While we were sinners Christ died for us. Jesus never sinned, but he became SIN by taking all our sins unto himself.

After he cried out these horrible words, Jesus said, "It is finished! Father, into your hands I give up my spirit!"

At that moment Jesus died. And the curtain of the temple between the Holy Place and the Holy of Holies, where the chief priest would go to sacrifice animals to pay the price for the sins of the people, was torn into two pieces by an invisible force. By this act, God was showing the whole world that no more sacrifices were needed for sin. His Son, Jesus, was to be the last sacrifice for sin the world would ever need.

All that God required after Jesus' death on the cross was for each person to believe and acknowledge that Jesus' death was the penalty paid for each person's sin. If Jesus didn't pay it, then people would have to pay it themselves.

A Roman soldier who had stood near the cross was the first to understand what Jesus did at that moment. When he heard Jesus' last words and saw how Jesus died, he said, "Truly this man was the Son of God."

All we like sheep have gone astray;

We have turned, every one, to his own way;

And the LORD has laid on Him the iniquity of us all.

ISAIAH 53:6

At the Tomb of Jesus

MATTHEW 27:57-28:10
MARK 16:1-13
LUKE 23:50-24:12
JOHN 19:38-20:18

J esus died on Friday afternoon. That evening a rich man named Joseph from the town of Arimathea went to Pilate's palace to ask if he could take down the body of Jesus and bury him. Pilate was surprised that Jesus had died after only six hours on the cross. Many people lingered for a day or two before they died. So Pilate called for a Roman soldier to confirm that Jesus had indeed died. When he learned that this was true, he gave orders to allow Joseph to take down the body from the cross and bury him.

So Joseph took the body of Jesus and wrapped it in fine linen cloth and placed the body in a new tomb that had been made for a wealthy man. Mary Magdalene and another woman named Mary watched as they laid Jesus' body in the cave-like tomb near a garden. Then Joseph ordered that a large stone be rolled over the tomb's entrance.

On Saturday morning some of the rulers of the Jews came to Pilate and said: "Sir, when this Jesus was alive he said that he would rise from the dead on the third day. We beg you to secure the tomb and post guards so that his disciples will not steal the body and tell everyone that he had indeed risen. This will be worse for us than when he was alive." Pilate agreed to seal the stone and sent soldiers to guard the entrance of the tomb. After they did this all was quiet for the rest of that day and night.

Very early on Sunday morning, the two women named Mary and a woman named Salome were on their way toward the tomb with fragrant perfumes to anoint Jesus' body. As they walked they asked each other, "Who will roll the great stone away from the front of the tomb?"

But when they came to the cave, they saw that the seal was broken, the stone was rolled away, and the soldiers who had been on guard were not there. Prior to their coming, there had been an earthquake followed by the appearance of an angel. When the soldiers felt the earthquake and saw the angel's dazzling light flashing in front of them, they fled in great fear. So the women came to an open tomb with the stone rolled to the side.

Mary Magdalene left to report this to the disciples. But the other Mary and Salome went into the tomb. Once inside they were filled with fear because they saw a young man dressed in a beautiful white garment.

"Do not be afraid," the angel said to them. "You are looking for Jesus who was crucified. He is not here; he is risen from the dead just as he said. See the place where they laid his body. He is not here. Now go and tell his disciples, and especially Peter, that Jesus will meet you in Galilee. You will see him there just as he promised." The women fled from the tomb.

While this was happening, Mary Magdalene went to tell Peter and John that the tomb was open. When she found them she said, "The tomb is open and they have taken the Lord out of the tomb. We do not know where they took the body!"

Peter and John ran to the tomb at once. When they arrived at the tomb they walked into the cave and saw long strips of linen cloth rolled up. But not finding the body, they went back into town to tell the other disciples.

Meanwhile, the guards reported to the religious leaders what they saw at the tomb. Then the leaders made up a story and gave the guards a lot of money to spread the word. "You are to report that his disciples came during the night and stole away the body while we were asleep."

So the soldiers took the money and did as they were instructed. And this story has been widely told to this very day.

When Mary Magdalene returned to the tomb the others had already gone. She wept as she sat there alone in front of the tomb thinking about the Lord's death on the cross. Now she was upset because no one knew where Jesus' body was.

Then she heard a voice say to her, "Woman, why do you weep?"

Thinking it was the gardener, she answered, "They have taken away my Lord, and I don't know where they have laid him. Sir, if you have carried him out of this place, tell me where you have laid him and I will take him away."

Then the voice spoke her name, "Mary!"

She knew at once that it was Jesus. He was no longer dead, but alive and standing right in front of her. She fell to the ground and cried out, "Master!"

Jesus said to her, "Do not touch me just yet. I must still go to my Father in heaven. But go to my brothers and tell them, 'I am going up to my Father and to your Father, to my God and your God!'"

Mary Magdalene did exactly as Jesus had told her. She hurried back and told the disciples, "I have seen the LORD!"

She was the first person to see Jesus after he had risen from the dead.

THE GREATEST DAY EVER

MATTHEW 28:16-20; LUKE 24: 13-53
JOHN 20: 24-31; ACTS 1:1-11
1 CORINTHIANS 15:3-8

After Jesus appeared to Mary Magdalene, he saw two of his followers walking from Jerusalem to a village called Emmaus, about seven miles away. He noticed that their faces were very sad, and he heard them discussing the news that the tomb of Jesus was empty and that no one knew where the body was. Jesus went up to them and asked, "What are you talking about?"

They did not recognize Jesus. One of them, Cleopas, was a little annoyed and said, "Do you not know about all the things that have happened in Jerusalem these past few days?"

"What things?" Jesus asked.

"About Jesus of Nazareth," Cleopas replied with his voice rising. "He was a great prophet who taught about God with powerful words and amazing miracles. We believed that he was the Messiah who was going to save Israel. But the chief priests and our leaders conspired to have him arrested and sentenced to death by crucifixion. That was three days ago. Now some of our women have just returned from the tomb and reported that they could not find his body. They said they had seen an angel who told them that he was alive. Some of our companions went to the tomb and found the tomb empty just as the women had said. But they, too, could not find the body."

For unto us a Child is born,

Unto us a Son is given;

And the government will be upon His shoulder.

And His name will be called

Wonderful, Counselor, Mighty God,

Everlasting Father, Prince of Peace.

Of the increase of His government and peace

There will be no end,

Upon the throne of David and over His kingdom,

To order it and establish it with judgment and justice

From that time forward, even forever.

The zeal of the Lord of hosts will perform this.

ISAIAH 9:6-7

Then Jesus said to them, "Did you not know that all this was predicted by the prophets? The one God sent had to suffer before going up to heaven." Then beginning with what Moses and all the Prophets had written in the Old Testament of the Bible, he explained to them all that was written about himself.

When they came to Emmaus the two men urged Jesus to have dinner with them. At the table Jesus took bread, gave thanks, broke it, and gave it to them. At that moment they recognized him as Jesus. Then he disappeared from their sight!

They were startled by this and asked, "Did not our hearts glow with joy as he explained the Bible to us?" That same night they hurried back to Jerusalem to report this to the other disciples. While they were talking, Jesus himself suddenly appeared and stood among them. He said, "Peace be with you."

They thought they were seeing a ghost, but Jesus calmed their fears. "Why are you frightened? Look at my hands and my feet. This is really me! Touch me and see. Does a ghost have flesh and bones, as you see I have?"

Then he told them, "This is what I said would happen. Everything that is written about me has been fulfilled."

Then Jesus opened their minds so they could understand the Bible. "The Christ had to suffer and rise from the dead so that repentance and forgiveness of sins in his name could be preached to people all over the world."

Over a period of forty days, Jesus appeared to the disciples many times, including five hundred people at one time. Then he led them again to the Mount of Olives and declared: "As my Father has sent me, so I send you. All power in heaven and on earth has been given to me. In a few days you will be baptized with the Holy Spirit. You will receive power when the Holy Spirit comes on you; and you will be my witnesses in Jerusalem, and in all Judea and Samaria, and to the ends of the earth. Go and preach this good news to every nation, baptizing them in the name of the Father and of the Son and of the Holy Spirit. Teach them to be my disciples. And know that I am with you always, even to the end of time."

After he said this, he was taken up to heaven, and a cloud hid him from his friends' sight. They watched Jesus disappear into the sky. Suddenly two angels stood beside them and said, "Why do you look into the sky? This Jesus, who has gone up into heaven, will also come back to you from heaven."

They returned to Jerusalem with great joy and happiness because they knew that one day Jesus would return with great power to rid the world completely of evil and sin. They prayed and worshiped God and prepared themselves to receive the Holy Spirit that Jesus had promised them, so that they could tell the world about Jesus.

The day Jesus rose from the dead was the greatest day the world has ever known. We call it Easter Sunday. And from that day forward every person who believes that Jesus is the Son of God can have their sins forgiven and receive the Holy Spirit in their lives. When they die they, too, will rise again to heaven and live forever with Jesus.

ABOUT THE AUTHOR

MAX MCLEAN has performed stories from the Bible to millions of people of all ages and from across religious and cultural spectra. He maintains an active performance schedule in theaters and houses of worship across America, and his radio program *Listen to the Bible* is heard daily on more than 650 radio outlets. He serves as president of the Fellowship for the Performing Arts. Max and his wife, Sharon, are the parents of two daughters.

FELLOWSHIP FOR THE PERFORMING ARTS (FPA) produces compelling theatre such as *Genesis* and *Mark's Gospel* that explore the events and characters that have made the Bible history's most enduringly powerful book. FPA also produces a line of audio and video products including *The Listener's Bible*, which was nominated by the Audio Publisher's Association (APA) for four Audie Awards, APA's highest honor.

For more information, visit: www.listenersbible.com or www.maxmclean.com